Oct., 1957

Florence Kelly Ashland

❧ MEMORIES ❧

ETHEL BARRYMORE
A Portrait by Sargent

MEMORIES

An Autobiography by

ETHEL BARRYMORE

ILLUSTRATED

HARPER & BROTHERS

New York

Contents

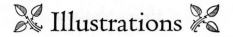 Illustrations

Illustrations

Miss Barrymore in *Rose Bernd*

In *The Second Mrs. Tanqueray*

The Lady of the Camellias

With Eva Le Gallienne in *L'Aiglon*

These illustrations will be found following page 238

Miss Barrymore in *The Kingdom of God*

Lionel, Ethel and John Barrymore in *Rasputin and the Empress*

The world première of the film at the Astor Theatre, New York

Ethel and John Barrymore with Diana Wynyard

Family gathering at the home of John Barrymore

Miss Barrymore in *The Corn Is Green*

Ethel Barrymore's 40th Anniversary Celebration

With Cary Grant in the film *None but the Lonely Heart*

Ethel Barrymore in 1946

Mrs. Eleanor Roosevelt presenting Miss Barrymore with the Barter Theatre Award

Ethel Barrymore's 70th birthday celebration

Miss Barrymore with Ethel Colt Miglietta and John Drew Miglietta at Mamaroneck

Reproductions in the text of theater programs, etc., were made possible through the courtesy of the Museum of the City of New York.

I

The Child One Was

The hardest thing is where to begin—or, perhaps, why? Well, I've read books and stories about us all, and none of them sounds quite right. So I am hoping this will at least give a flavor of this family that has lived for generations in a series of goldfish bowls, completely obscured by myths and legends.

I'll begin with my grandmother, the mother of my mother. She was born in a village in Kent amidst the rogues and vagabonds that she loved and honored by her genius and grandeur through seventy-five years on the stage. Her name was Louisa Lane, and she was brought to America as a little girl by her mother, my great-grandmother, and *her* name was Mrs. Eliza Kinloch. Don't ask me why they had different names—I never dared to ask.

So many things were considered impertinences in our family. I was made aware of this at a very early age. Nothing was ever said . . . you simply knew.

Grandma Kinloch found New York a noisy and vulgar place. So they took coach to Philadelphia, which they found charming, and there they stayed.

There is a program announcing "Mrs. Eliza Kinloch, a Sweet Singer of Ballads." And endless programs of Miss Lane as Richard the Third!!! And a play called *Twelve Precisely* in which Miss Lane played five characters, two young gentlemen and three young ladies. There are many more . . . and then she was Mrs. Hunt, playing Shakespeare and all the classics. Then she was Mrs. Mossop, I think rather briefly . . . still playing everything. Then suddenly the

3

important marriage to my grandfather, John Drew, an Irish actor who, I've been told, was brilliant and of an enormous fascination. She proceeded to have four children: my Aunt Louisa, my Uncle John, my mother and Sidney. Uncle Sidney may not have been the son of John Drew, but he was indubitably the son of Mrs. John Drew.

My grandfather died when he was less than thirty-five years old. The only thing of interest I can remember being told—and that by an ancient family retainer—was that after the birth of my mother, he was "allowed" to go on an Australian tour; and with him, as his leading lady, was a young sister of my grandmother's (where she was born or why I've never learned). Her name was Georgiana and 'tis said Grandfather had fallen in love with her and had wished to marry her. But my more forceful grandmother had said, "Nonsense!" and married him herself. When they came back to Philadelphia from Australia, there was a tiny girl with them whom my grandmother adopted and called Adine Stevens. We called her Aunt Tibby and loved her dearly. She was a sweet, gentle creature with a lovely voice, who went about quietly helping everyone, and died in her early twenties.

My Aunt Louisa I never knew. She married Charles Mendum, who managed the Arch Street Theatre for the lessee and manageress, Mrs. John Drew—and was promptly fired for presuming. At any rate, they went to live in Boston where Mr. Mendum, Sr., was a banker—a kindly man, whose house, I detect, had a roof. My two cousins, Edmund and Georgia Mendum, I didn't see until we were fifteen or sixteen years old. And by then my Aunt Louisa had died. She had never been on the stage.

There is so much to be written about my cousins Georgie and Ed—two brilliant creatures. Ed dismissed the stage as a livelihood with hauteur, worked his way to Europe, wandered all over it on foot; then did the same thing over a good part of Asia; came home and wrote a sardonic book called *The Barbarian* and became a newspaperman.

Georgie must be brought in and kept in—later.

But to return to Philadelphia: Mrs. John Drew had established at the Arch Street Theatre an exceptionally fine stock company—and at home an exceptionally rigid and appallingly respectable household.

I remember hearing my mother say that if she were allowed to have a young man in to tea, "Mother sat at the other end of the drawing room snowing on us."

Mrs. Drew was a pillar of St. Stephen's Episcopal Church and her son John went to the Episcopal Academy; and my mother Georgie had a Sunday-school class. But they were people of infinite gaiety and humor, and were forever untouched by the severity of their upbringing. I have always suspected that my grandmother had a twinkle in her eye, even in her most awesome moments.

Then John wanted to go on the stage. So off to the Arch Street Theatre where, to serve his apprenticeship, he appeared first in a one-act play, *Cool as a Cucumber*—not in the general repertoire but, I suppose, as a test; then was trusted with various small parts; and then—I daresay with the idea of getting out from under—he went to New York and joined Augustin Daly's very important company.

My mother, Georgie, by this time had begun playing her small parts at the Arch Street Theatre. And one Sunday John came to spend the day in Philadelphia, bringing with him a spectacular young Englishman who was also starting an acting career with the Daly company. His name was Maurice Barrymore—and that was indeed that! He had been born in the dungeons of the Fort of Agra in India during the Mutiny, where my paternal grandfather was in the British Civil Service, a judge. He was the youngest child. My Aunt Beatrix, the eldest, married General Angelo of the Indian Army; and Aunt Eva married one Wace who was in the Civil Service and whose brother was the Dean of Canterbury. Their name was Blyth.

Young Herbert Maurice Blyth was sent home to England at the usual age—about eight—and went to a preparatory school at Blackheath, then to Harrow, and then to Cambridge, where he became amateur champion boxer of England. Then he began to read for the bar, ate his dinners, etc. Then came upon the scene two villains—or angels—who told him it would be years before he would get a brief, and—"Look at him! And listen to that voice!—the stage!" He was flattered and delighted, and broke it to his family, who recoiled in horror as only Victorian Anglo-Indians could. So he gaily promised to find another name and do his damnedest in America. And if he failed, he would come home, resume his role of barrister and become a Q.C. So off he went, with his beauty, his charm, and his wit to conquer the new world and make his fortune.

What a magic flame was lighted that Sunday in a small house in Philadelphia!—that lovely, fair-gallant girl and that overwhelming and unpredictable Briton, my mother and father to be. I don't know how many Sunday visits before they were engaged . . . I should think not many. And then they were married.

There is much written today about Command Performances. Well, my mother made three—all in my grandmother's house in Philadelphia, and their names were Lionel, Ethel and John.

It must be understood that there was never any money anywhere that wasn't earned week by week by this whole family by the profession of acting; except by my grandmother's Arch Street Theatre which she leased and managed for many years—sometimes acting but always managing. So it was in Philadelphia that she had her house, and it was unthinkable that her daughter's children should be born anywhere else. It was a command tempered by sense and a quiet, unspoken feeling. That house was our home as little children. In fact, it was the only home we ever knew together. We were to be separated very early in our lives by various circumstances. Consequently, when we met later in life we were rather formal with each other and very, very polite. It appears that rather terrified observers. I remember Lionel telling me that a friend of his who was present when I dined with him once said to him, "My God! Don't you know each other?"

One may write about the child one was with the same freedom that a novelist creates a character. There is no fear of egotism, for the portrait is one of faint colors, and the incidents that crowd in on any small life are incidents of childhood rather than of a particular child. I see myself a shy little figure against the background of a family group whose vivacity was that of my mother and father, whose stronger, darker, more frequent moods were those of my grandmother.

I was brought up in the interim of busy lives, lives of the theater, where children had to be set aside and cared for by others, so my most vivid memories of the beginning are naturally those connected with the rare times when the family were together. If I speak of my elders a great deal in these early years it is, first of all, because I had a remarkable grandmother and because my parents had a romantic glamour about them which appealed to a child.

I have never met anyone who had quite the amazing force without effort that my grandmother possessed. Her supreme rule at the theater crystallized into certain ceremonials that marked her comings and goings. She would drive from home in her brougham, and when she reached her office she would go over books, listen to reports, sign documents and inspect things with that regal manner which betokens state affairs. And as she rose to leave, it seemed as though a red carpet should have been spread before her. When, in later years, I saw royalty abroad, nothing was a surprise to me—I had seen my grandmother.

To her the theater was never "show business." My grandmother would rise up out of her grave if she heard me use that word. She'd say "show—do you mean a circus?" and she would say it as if she were the Red Queen saying, "Off with her head!"

She used to have dinner in Philadelphia at three o'clock,

a cup of tea just before going to the theater and perhaps supper or a cup of soup afterward. We called her Mummum (with the accent on the last syllable), which was probably invented by Lionel, as he was the eldest. And my father always addressed her as Ma'am—like royalty, which, I must say, she received with equanimity. I feel that she regarded him as a person, with an amused and affectionate tolerance, and as an actor, a gifted amateur. According to her, one didn't spring equipped for the fray from either the Inner Temple or the British Civil Service. My mother she adored, though there was never any demonstration.

I thought that house in Twelfth Street was enormous—with large rooms and cavernous halls and most alarming echoes. I can see now the Victorian landscapes on the wall, the gold-colored sofa, the music box on the table which Grandmother magnificently wound up so that it might unwind "The Carnival of Venice," and the square piano upon which were pictures of Edwin Forrest and his wife. There was a sturdy solemnity about the place which made me seem very tiny. Years later when I went back, somehow the house appeared to have shrunk. Everyone has experienced the same thing, I suppose. I sought, with some echo of the alarm I used to feel, for a copy of *The Ancient Mariner*, once so big that I could scarcely hold it on my lap, but it was only of ordinary size.

But about the house: on the second floor there was the sitting room, then the bathroom, and then the annex, which was our playroom. Then there was the big front bedroom which was a little frightening to pass, for in it dwelt my

great-grandmother, who was ninety-five. There was nothing
on earth to be frightened about . . . perhaps it was the
deference and attention Mummum paid her, and Aunt
Tibby flying to answer her bell. Grandma Kinloch was very
nice to us in a vague, unaware sort of way, but I always felt
a little terror.

Then there was the long flight up to the third floor, rather
dark at night. I remember Jack being made to go up it alone
as a very little boy. As he disappeared in the darkness he was
heard to say, "You can't hurt me. I have a wonderful power!"

So that was our home when our parents were on the road
or in New York, which I'm sure my grandmother spoke of
as "out of town." On the ground floor also was the kitchen,
which held charm and mystery for us because we were never
allowed to go into it. Such beautiful smells! And soft Irish
laughter. We always had Irish cooks and maids—all known
as Mary Aggie. I suppose there once had been a Mary Aggie.
Then there was Lily Garrett, Mummum's dresser, always
known, for some obscure reason, as "the pearl-handled
knife." And her mother, Mrs. Garrett, who took home to her
house our laundry. And Kitty, her daughter-in-law, who was
our nurse. Kitty once took Lionel and me to see Mrs. Garrett
and left us for a moment in the yard. There was a round
wooden washtub on the grass, filled with heavenly blue,
blue water. We were both sitting in it in our best clothes
when she came out. Poor Kitty! (The Garretts were not
Irish; they were pure Philadelphia.)

I can't say what my earliest recollections were specifically.
Those things, as Mrs. Malaprop declares, were a long time
ago "illiterated" from my memory. I do know, in her words

again, that at no period was I a "progeny of learning," but seem to have been a normal, healthy child in spirits, ably seconded and sometimes led by my brothers. I often wonder what those days would have been had I really known my mother well. I have only intermittent pictures of her—a tall, fair, slender girl with blue eyes. I looked at her in worship and in silence, longing to talk with her, but fearing, out of the very shyness of my nature, to speak to her.

My father, of course, had really startling beauty. My brother Jack looked exactly like him—as the image at the small end of the telescope is like the one at the other. When Papa first came from England he had the eyeglass, the tall hat—all the marks of fashion of those days. Later he became perfectly appalling in his clothes; I will never know why, but he seemed to have a kind of mania to shock.

We were a mischievous set of children, always up to some adventure. My memory brings to view many wiggling moments. If in the presence of our elders we were not allowed "to utter"—our grandmother's way of condensing the golden injunction that children should be seen but not heard—when we were together we "uttered" loudly and continuously.

We were always falling into something or out of something. One summer Jack dropped from a tree on a flower pot and cut his head. He always had the slight scar. And I vividly recall a fishing expedition Lionel and I took, with our lines hung over the third-floor baluster rail of the house on Twelfth Street. We could see them dangling all the way down to the entrance hall. In the anxiety to keep my line free from Lionel's, I leaned too far and down I went the three flights through the open space between the balusters. I lay there still and without a cry. The air was torn by the frantic shouts of Aunt Tibby, who had been in the dining room doing something with strawberries. She had seen the drop and she did not expect that I would be alive. A cab was sent post haste for Doctor Mitchell, who had brought us into the world. And by some miracle—children, it seems, are watched over by a miraculous spirit—I was found to be safe and sound.

Occasionally Mummum would go on a tour and then Mrs. Griffiths was with us. I remember asking the current Mary Aggie who she was. "Housekeeper!" she said, rather bitterly. She was a perfectly pleasant person and took us one Sunday to midday dinner with her daughter in Darby, and she gave us that marvelous Philadelphia epic, Dexter's White Mountain Cake! Think of all the millions of be-nighted people in the world who don't know about Dexter's White Mountain Cake.

There came a magic day when Lionel and I were packed up and taken by our father and mother to a private car where we were welcomed by what I now know to be the most charming and entrancing woman I was ever to meet. She was Madame Modjeska. Papa was to play Romeo, Orlando, Armand, etc., and Mamma was what was called the leading lady to a feminine star. I was only four years old, but I re-member Madame as Rosalind and Marguerite Gautier more vividly than any memory of Duse, Bernhardt, Réjane, or Ellen Terry. I don't remember Papa or Mamma in the plays at all. But Madame Modjeska was stamped on my mind and heart indelibly for my life, and my gratitude is unbounded. Both my parents worshiped her. She was a devout Catholic, and as the months went by Mamma became more and more sure she must be a Catholic, too. So suddenly Lionel and I were surprised to be baptized again. Madame Modjeska and her husband, Count Bozenta, were Lionel's godparents; and Miss Veronica Murray, who presided over a very elegant boardinghouse in New York, and one Perugini, the only Catholic Mamma could find at the moment, were mine. Jack, who was only two at this time, had been left at home with Mummum, so escaped for the time being. Father was infinitely amused by all this, but I'm afraid Mummum was shocked and horrified. Words like "Papists," etc., escaped her. But when we—Lionel and I—got back to Philadelphia, she could detect no ghastly difference . . . until much later when we went to school, when she gave tongue; and for a brief moment was under the impression that she and Papa had something important in common—one of her incredibly few errors.

Lionel and I were taken on that tour because Madame Modjeska had her own private car and she invited Mamma and Papa to be her guests and also Lionel and me. I remember Mamma sitting in the car smocking a dress for me. And I can see Lionel now, sprawling flat on his stomach in the aisle, drawing ships and trains, as we traveled from place to place.

After that wonderful tour with Madame Modjeska we came home to "The Tomb of the Capulets," Mamma's name for Mummum's house—partly, I suppose, because down the street there was a man who made headstones and partly a humorous allusion to slight family differences between Uncle Jack and Uncle Sidney. About this time my father fell heir to some money left him by one of those inevitable English aunts so popular and obliging in that era of Victorian fiction. Because of this we went to England, where we remained for two years.

Everything about those two years was magical. Those London days are clear and shiny in my mind. Our house was in St. John's Wood Road, with a garden surrounded by a tall brick wall. From our nursery at the back of the house on the third floor we could see Lord's cricket ground where all the most famous matches were played. We used to borrow father's field glasses and try to watch the matches. We had a lovely big garden and a great many animals—dogs and monkeys. Papa loved monkeys and birds. The monkeys were kept in cages in the very large garden.

We also had a nurse named Polly. I remember that she had crinkly red hair and that Papa said she looked like Mary Anderson only more beautiful. She took us everywhere —even to the Chamber of Horrors at Madame Tussaud's, which remembrance caused me to wake up screaming for years afterward.

I was a shy little mortal, with large eyes cast down in continual agonizing bashfulness. At such times my father or mother would call out to me, "Look up, Pauline," a line from *The Lady of Lyons*. Everything was a quotation in our household. At the table it seemed as though we could never get away from famous lines. If we had to go to bed, it was "Stand not upon the order of your going, but go at once!"

If we hurried through our meals, we were admonished to eat "wisely and slow."

In London Papa was playing at the Haymarket Theatre in *Diplomacy* (Sardou) and in *A Woman of No Importance* (Wilde).

Mamma was usually "at home" Sunday afternoons, and I used to be produced at teatime to hand about cakes, etc.—always with my eyes firmly on the ground. Once as I approached a gentleman sitting on the sofa, Mamma called to me, "Look up, Pauline!"—which I did, shrieked in terror, dropped the plate, and fled to the third floor. The man was Oscar Wilde. My parents nearly killed me. I don't remember ever being so severely punished for anything. There was something in the family known as the Green Slipper. It was made of soft Russian leather, and had been one of Mummum's bedroom slippers. The mere mention of it terrified us . . . I doubt if it would have hurt a fly. It had a very complete workout that awful day.

Everything else, though, was lovely. I remember a children's party, with Lionel encased in a blue velvet suit and a perfect fury—which wasn't mitigated by a small boy shrilling at him "Barrymore, you're fetched!" when Polly came for us. That became a family wheeze. I hope I can remember half of our family wheezes.

Then back to Philadelphia to Mummum. Lionel and I by then sounded like two English children. When we returned home all the famous legacy had been blown—but Polly came with us. She soon married the livery-stable man where Mummum kept her brougham. He got drunk every

Saturday night and beat her up—Mamma remarking, "She might as well have stayed at home!"

Then Kitty came back to us and, as time passed, presented several complaints to Mummum, one of which was that "Mr. Lionel was very naughty, Mrs. Drew."

"Well, what did he do?"

"He kicked me, Mrs. Drew. He kicked me in the shins."

"Shins, woman!" thundered Mummum. "What are shins? Leave the room!"

It was suddenly decided that we should be sent to boarding school. I was sent to the Academy of Notre Dame in Philadelphia, and Lionel to Mount St. Vincent on the Hudson. Jack stayed at home with Mummum.

My first months at the convent were easier than Lionel's at his school. The older girls, during recess, would put me on the end of a bench and ask questions, and would scream with joy at my very English answers. Lionel was having an awful time with his accent—the boys calling him "Lord Cornwallis" and making his life miserable. He ran away twice from that school, walking through the tunnel into the old Grand Central Station. No flashlights then—in fact, no *nothing*—except monstrous trains bearing down on a small boy in the blackness.

Entirely apart from my success as a comic exponent of the English language at the age of six, I loved the convent. The sisters were extraordinarily understanding, kind and helpful —especially when my life became difficult later on.

I was six when I was sent to the convent and I was there until I was twelve. Of course I had many weekends at home

with Mummum and specially wonderful ones when Mamma
would come on Sunday. Occasionally Papa might be there,
too. In those days I wore heavy bangs—and how much he
disliked them. He used to push my hair back and say it
should be like "Alice's" with a round comb. This made me
burst into tears because I didn't want to be different from
the other girls. I won the argument—but how right he was!

So I lived the routine of a convent boarder, and since I
was one of the youngest, the sisters called me "Little Ethel."
Many years later I visited my old music teacher in Dayton,
Ohio, where she had been transferred and I was still "Little
Ethel."

Sister Aloysius was a great music teacher—strict and very
tough—who stood no nonsense, was almost impossible to
please. I got my silver medal for playing Beethoven's Sonata
No. 13 but she saw to it that May Heizmann from Reading,
Pennsylvania, got the first prize for playing "Nearer My
God to Thee" with variations—very salutary.

In a general way my father knew what his daughter was
"taking" at the convent, but how well it was taking did not
dawn upon him until one Sunday afternoon when Mummum summoned him to hear me play. He stood by and,
as I looked up when I had finished, I could see that there
were tears in his eyes.

He said, "Vienna, Leschetizky—she must go—"

I was thrilled and never heard of it again.

In the classrooms I suffered much because of my shyness.
Whenever we were told to memorize anything for our
English class and had to stand up and say it the next day,
I had my full quota of torture. The ease with which so many

of the children rattled off Shakespeare was a constant source of wonderment to me. The confidence of the amateur was not mine.

Sometimes on Saturday afternoon we would be taken to a matinee at the Arch Street Theatre. The building had pillars outside like the old Greek Parthenon and inside it was all red velvet and gold, as I think all theaters should be. We sat in a box marked "D" and only Mummum had the key.

We were taught firmly as children that whenever any member of the family appeared on the stage we were never to applaud. Never! It just wasn't done, either when they came on the stage or at the end of the performance. To do so would have been to break one of the firmest family rules of etiquette.

I remember one play called *A Parlor Match* by Charles Hoyt principally because there was a lovely little girl in the cast called "The Innocent Kid" whom I believed to be just my age. She had black silk stockings and long golden curls and an enchanting little red dress. We were taken backstage to meet the stars—Evans and Hoey—and "The Innocent Kid" turned out to be Mrs. Evans! I cried all the way home.

It was during these days that the magnitude of my grandmother most struck me. Her power seemed to exude from her regal presence; she was commanding. I believe she unbent more to Jack than to anyone; her love for him was of the tender kind. Yet she never allowed any advantage to be taken of such sentiment on her part. One day Jack was late for a meal. He rushed in, out of breath, with an evident plan of attack.

"Oh, Mummum," he exclaimed in an awe-stricken voice, "have you ever seen a house all painted black?"

"No," she said abruptly, "nor have you. Sit down."

Mummum would never allow us to be late for anything —it was just not heard of. You can't ever be late in the theater; punctuality is part of it, and it was part of our life in Mummum's house. It has always been part of my life, and I have no patience with late people, especially not with those who take a great deal of trouble to be late.

Those Sundays when Mamma was playing in New York and could come to spend the day with us were a great thrill. I didn't feel that I knew her very well, but she was very gay and made me laugh a lot. I didn't know then that she was known as a truly witty woman.

Charles Frohman told me long afterward that once when Mamma was on tour in one of his companies she telegraphed him from San Francisco that she needed new clothes for the play and he telegraphed back one word, "No."

My mother telegraphed "Oh."

And he was so delighted that she got the clothes.

Jack by now was old enough to go to kindergarten, and there was a little boys' school on Twentieth Street at the end of our convent garden, presided over by Sister Vincent, who looked like a cheerful red apple. She adored Jack and I am sure spared him all trials and tribulations. He was a day scholar and went home to Mummum in the afternoon.

Then he and Lionel were sent to Seton Hall, a Jesuit school in New Jersey. Poor Mummum! All these Catholic schools and now Jesuits!

Jack could always manage to upset the family by mar-

velous stories of things happening to him. When he was at
Seton Hall he wrote an impassioned letter to Grandmother,
telling her how one of the priests had "felled me to the
ground with a blow." The Episcopal side of our family
smiled in the midst of their horror. And it was decided that
my father should go down from New York where he was
playing at the time and investigate the matter.

He, metaphorically rolling up his sleeves, said, "Ma'am!
Leave it to me!" and off he went to New Jersey to wipe up
the entire school. Jack, lurking in the hall, saw him storm
into the headmaster's study, where he remained about three
hours, emerging wreathed in smiles, declaring to all and
sundry, including Jack, "Nonsense, my boy! Most charming man I ever met," dashed for a train and was late for his
performance. I believe they'd been discussing the Carlisle
Harris murder case, and had had a wonderful time.

In the summer, vacations were spent in various places.
Sometimes we were joined by Uncle Googan—he was Sidney Drew. He was very gay and, I daresay, very naughty
and generally beguiling. I think Mummum was greatly
relieved when he married Aunt Gladys, as she was young,
beautiful and very haughty. Also, she was the daughter of
McKee Rankin, a well-known actor of whom Mummum
approved.

The summer when I was eight we had a house at Fort
Wadsworth, Staten Island—or rather, it was a small boardinghouse, Madame Bourquin's, which our family almost
entirely monopolized. We lived out of doors most of the
time. Devoured by mosquitoes, I was a perfect tattoo of
bites. Because of these marks, they spoke of me as "the

leopard child." I was also known as "the water rat." I would dare anything in the water, and in one of my mad adventures I came near drowning at Quarantine.

Then there was a summer at Pleasure Bay where Lionel and Jack built a catamaran which sank under them in the middle of the Shrewsbury River, and cheering crowds from both sides of the river leaped in to save two small, very good swimmers.

Sometimes Papa and Mamma were with us—not often. They were off on tour, sometimes together, sometimes not. But how wonderful it was to see Mamma diving through great breakers and then run laughing so gaily to us along the beach, calling, "Come along, Kids—lunch!" It was lovely to hear her say "Kids."

Once when I was about ten Mummum took me with her on a visit to Mr. Joseph Jefferson at his house on Buzzard's Bay. The only part I had ever seen Mummum play was Mrs. Malaprop and always with Mr. Jefferson as Bob Acres. I used to think *The Rivals* was the only important play in the world. One evening after dinner Mummum and Mr. Jefferson were sitting on the porch, rocking and reminiscing, when he said, "Don't you think so, Louisa?" She said, "Yes. You know, Joseph, you are the only one left who calls me Louisa."

And I burst into loud tears. It seemed to me so sad. Mummum turned on me in amazed indignation, when I was saved by a voice floating across the bay.

"Coming fishing in the morning, Joseph?"

"No, Grover. Mrs. Drew is spending a few days with me."

"Oh! My respects, Madame."

On the way upstairs to bed I asked, "Who was the fat man in the boat, Mummum?"

Then I really did *get* it. Apparently one did not refer to the President of the United States as "the fat man in the boat."

I must dwell a little more on the Convent of Notre Dame on Rittenhouse Square in Philadelphia. It is a Belgian order, with its Mother House in Namur. I like to think of three wonderful women: the Sister Superior Agnes Mary, Sister Aloysius, my piano teacher, and Sister Julie de St. Esprit, who was mistress of the boarders when I was there and whose duty it was to know all about us—and I mean *all*. And she never failed in that duty. I owe her so much. I was never able to repay her because it was only late in my life that I realized that before any spiritual or moral lapses I might have considered, I would pause, for somewhere in the distance or maybe by my shoulder like a guardian angel, there was Sister Julie saying, "Really, Ethel, don't be absurd!"

Sister Superior Agnes Mary was a gentle, saintly woman —more of her later.

There were a few months when Mamma and Papa rented Uncle Jack's apartment in New York when he and his family (Aunt Dodo and Bee, their daughter) were abroad; and I was there part of a vacation. And that was when Papa took me to my first baseball game. I was about seven years old. We went to the old Polo Grounds on the elevated railroad. I was very excited but not nearly as excited as my father. It turned out that he was a Giant fan, which I have

Ethel Barrymore (photo by Offner, Spencer Berger Collection)

John Drew, Sr., grandfather of Ethel Barrymore (Spencer Berger Collection)

Mrs. Drew's Arch Street Theatre, Philadelphia (Culver Service)

Mrs. John Drew as Mrs. Malaprop (Spencer Berger Collection)

John Drew (Uncle Jack)

Mr. and Mrs. Sidney Drew—Uncle Googan and
Gladys Rankin (Spencer Berger Collection)

John Drew and Billie Burke in *My Wife*
(Culver Service)

Georgie Drew Barrymore and her children, Ethel, Lionel and John (Spencer Berger Collection)

Mrs. John Drew, Sr., and Georgie Drew (Culver Service)

Georgie Drew Barrymore (Spencer Berger Collection)

Maurice Barrymore, father of Ethel
(Spencer Berger Collection)

Ethel Barrymore at about the age of ten (upper left), two youthful pictures, and (lower right) in the costume she wore in *His Excellency, the Governor* (Culver Service)

Sir Henry Irving and Ellen Terry in
Madison, Wisconsin (Culver Service)

Helena Modjeska (Culver Service)

Sir James M. Barrie

William Gillette

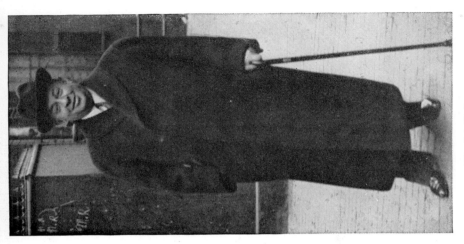

Charles Frohman

An early picture of Maude Adams and Ethel Barrymore, taken in Springfield, Massachusetts (Photo by W. W. Bellows, Bosworth Studio)

found out during the years is not the same as being a base-ball fan. Well, this day the Giants lost, and my father couldn't have been more agonized. He walked violently up and down the platform, throwing his arms to heaven, say-ing, "God! how could you do this to me, how could you?" I slipped into another car in the train, pretending I didn't know that eccentric Englishman—and I can't tell you how English he sounded in the shadow of Coogan's Bluff. I had no idea where to get off that elevated train, so I was even-tually removed to a police station and returned rather in style to my parents and the green slipper. It was later that I learned to love baseball, but I never, never had a favorite team!

It is strange to think of the difference in behavior of my father, coming from the sort of family he did, and the family into which he married. He was, of course, intensely emo-tional and what is now called uninhibited. So, in a way, are we. But such is the powerful and lingering influence of my grandmother, our deepest feelings are never to be disclosed. They are our own private affairs, never to be paraded in public. Strong emotions—either sad or glad—may be hurled with gusto at an audience, with the footlights in between—and then we are being not ourselves, but an author's inven-tion that we leave at the stage door, like the key of our dressing room. I have never heard of any Drew doing a recitation and I know we children never did. And I always hated charades and "the game" where you had to act out various words! I have often fled a house when they insisted how good I would be.

The school terms passed one by one. I was always prac-

ticing the piano and poring over books. On my occasional
visits home during rare weekends I would get hold of *David
Greve* or *Robert Elsmere* and read and read and read. I
would never go out unless I was almost hurled out.

When I was thirteen years old I was suddenly taken from
the convent and sent to New York to my mother. She was
ill—bronchitis they said—and was to be sent to California
and I was to go with her. We were to go by boat down to
the Isthmus of Panama, across it in a train, then up the
Pacific to Santa Barbara, where Mamma was to get well.
It was all very exciting, and I kept hoping I would be all
right and not too shy or scared. It was bad just before the
boat sailed when Mamma was saying good-by to Papa and
begging him not to forget her. It was my first sight of
tragedy, although I didn't know it then.

I slept in the upper berth of that little cabin and one
night I woke up to hear Mamma crying and saying over and
over, "What's going to happen to my three kids!" I felt a sort
of terror, but also felt I mustn't let her know I had heard.
Then she coughed and coughed—not loud, rather gently—
and then she fell asleep.

I stood on the back platform of the train crossing Panama,
fascinated by the great deserted machines of the de Lesseps
attempt sinking into the ground . . . then the other boat,
stopping at several little Mexican ports . . . and then Santa
Barbara, one night at the Arlington Hotel . . . then the
lovely little house covered with roses even all over the roof
and pouring into my window. And the great and wonderful
gentleman who was our Chinese cook . . . and everything
else.

Mamma, of course, had a letter to the doctor who was going to make her well. He was a great, tall man with a red beard, wise and kind. After he had listened to Mamma's chest and heard her cough, I remember he said, "Yes—and who is taking care of you, Mrs. Barrymore?" and she said, "My little girl." And then he looked very grave and said, "You have no nurse?" And she laughed and said, "Oh no, I don't want a nurse . . . just my little girl." And he said, "Yes, she will take good care of you." And I was frightened.

Mamma had brought all her clothes with her and I spent some happy hours upstairs in a big room with huge cupboards unpacking them. Lovely brocade evening dresses and brocade evening shoes . . . I really think she had brought all the possessions she had in the world.

People in Santa Barbara were very friendly and called on Mamma, and one Sunday morning the mayor was to take her for a drive. When I brought in her breakfast that morning she was very gay and said how well she felt and that I must run off to mass, as she knew how much I wanted to, so I did. And I was walking slowly home in the middle of the road, kicking stones and every now and then doing a little dance, when I saw a girl running toward me. It was Mabel, the mayor's daughter. She called to me "Oh Ethel! Hurry home, your mother has had a hemorrhage." I got home just before she died. She didn't know me. She was thirty-four and a great and gallant lady, my beloved mother whom I hardly knew.

The dreadful days that followed were made livable by great kindnesses. First there was our Chinaman who, saying, "Little Missy must not see," had made my dear mother

and her room look as if no terrible thing had happened. I
sent a telegram to my father and to Uncle Sidney to tell
Mummum and my brothers. And then I ordered my black
dress—a grown-up dress—and put up my hair. Then there
was the undertaker and all the arrangements to be made, as
I was to take Mamma back to Philadelphia and poor Mummum. I suppose I was in a state of shock because I didn't cry
very much until I began packing all the lovely clothes and
all the lovely shoes. Then I cried and cried, and our dear
Chinaman brought me a cup of tea and patted my shoulder
and went away . . . so wise, so helpful. And the mayor and
his wife and some kind people named Dibblee, and others
who helped me. I've been grateful to them all my life.
Madame Modjeska met me in Los Angeles—she and her
husband—and they helped me. Poor Madame couldn't stop
crying, though she tried so hard to, and I felt I had to comfort her. Then I was in my lower berth in my long black
dress, and thought, "Next month I'll be fourteen."

❧ II ❧

A Time of Searching

I went back to the convent in September. The two important things I remember about that year were, first, that I discovered Jack had not been baptized a Catholic when Lionel and I were. I found a boy at Sister Vincent's school who looked quite old. He was, I think, twelve, and his name was Sam McGargle. He assented after much agonized pressure to be Jack's godfather and I was his godmother. The ceremony was at St. Patrick's near the convent and must have presented a fantastic picture, and I daresay I felt like St. Paul or at any rate Bishop Sheen.

The other important thing was when the Superior sent for me and gave me a cutting from a newspaper. My father was married again, and she had not wanted me to hear of it from one of the day scholars. I do not want to dwell too much on this, but it was years, really years, before I could take it in stride.

There were beginning to be quite a lot of things to be taken in stride. In June I was sent for by Mummum to join her and Uncle Sidney in Montreal to go on the stage. I had never known I was to go on the stage. I had thought I was going to be a great pianist, with fine dreams of Vienna and Leschetizky. But suddenly there was no money, no Arch Street Theatre, no house, and I must earn my living. No one talked about it; no one talked about it at all, ever.

I was given a scene to learn in *The Rivals*. Mr. Jefferson, in his acting version of *The Rivals*, had always omitted the part of Julia, but I was told that it was to be put back and given to me for my debut. It was a small scene in the first

act, with Aunt Gladys, who was Lydia Languish, and it
could be removed easily from the play the next night if I
proved myself inadequate.

On the first night I had on more make-up than I have
ever used in all the years since. Mummum sent for me.
She looked at me and said, "What have you got on your
face?"

I said, "Make-up."

She said, "Go and wash it all off."

So I did. I don't know where I had got the idea you had
to put on a lot of make-up. Nobody had ever told me anything about it, and I had never seen anyone make up.

On the stage that first night before an audience I was
naturally terrified. But when Aunt Gladys (who had never
played the scene before) and I sat facing each other on a
little sofa and I saw that unforgettable glazed, almost idiotic
look on her face—a look only to be found on an actress's
face when she hasn't the faintest idea of what her lines are
—I found myself asking myself questions and answering
them briskly in my best elementary-school manner. How
absurd I must have been, and how awfully unlike "A Young
Lady of Fashion" by Richard Brinsley Sheridan.

But there I was, on the stage with Mummum and Uncle
Sidney, and so began an apprenticeship which was to last
for more than half a century. I don't remember ever being
told anything by anyone. Once when I did ask Mummum
something about acting, she lifted her eyebrows and said,
"You should know that without being told." It always
seemed to be taken for granted that I would know what to

do without being told. Of course I didn't. Luckily the parts given to me were tiny, so I didn't ruin anything.

There was some talk of doing another play. I remember Uncle Sidney's saying, "But who would do the young girl's part?" And Mummum saying, "Ethel," and Sidney laughing and saying, "Mother, I know we come from a family who kill (Defarge in *A Tale of Two Cities*) but not yet!"

After a few weeks in Montreal, Mummum left for New York, turning me over to my uncle. Mrs. Rankin, Gladys's mother, arrived—which meant different plays with no parts for me. So, often, if there was a piano in the orchestra pit, I played it between the acts and enjoyed myself a lot.

And one unforgettable Saturday night in St. John's, New Brunswick, we stayed in the theater in the dark until after midnight. Then, as it was Sunday, we strolled out and onto a train for other parts. All our luggage had to be left in the hotel and my trunk containing all my worldly possessions —not many really—I didn't see for years. I remember Aunt Gladys leaving the theater that night looking very proud and grand, also rather fat. She had on five dresses.

After that we played a week in Halifax. The manager insisted on our doing another play, besides the three we had been doing; and Mrs. Rankin insisted on *Oliver Twist* because she was a famous Nancy Sikes. Uncle Googan went out and bought a Samuel French paper-bound copy of it. He played Fagin. There wasn't time for him to learn the part and he didn't know a word of it, but he gave a wonderful performance just the same. He wore a funny little red beard and called everybody Nancy, my dear, no matter whom he was talking to. I played Rose Maylie, and I had to meet Nancy at London Bridge. They threw a green light on her. She looked so frightening that I forgot every word.

As I remember it now, I received no salary; I suppose my uncle thought it would recompense me if my meager hotel bills were paid. Being new to this kind of life, I traveled around in a continual state of excitement. After Halifax we played Bar Harbor for one night. I wasn't in the play, so between the acts I went down in the orchestra and played the piano. Bar Harbor was full of people from Philadelphia, and a lot of the girls I knew there came up and talked to me.

We were to go to Bangor the next day for two nights, and Uncle Googan thought it would be nice to charter a little pleasure launch to go there. We were all delighted because we had heard that the fleet was in at Bangor and the house was completely sold out. We were looking forward to a theater full of uniforms with all the boxes filled with admirals and their ladies. We started in beautiful weather but we had not been out from shore for long before a dense fog settled upon us in a thick blanket and we suddenly realized that no one on board could tell exactly where we were going or where we were. It also developed that the captain of the launch had no charts and knew no more than we where we were going or where we were.

We felt our way very slowly, and from the sounds of the great foghorns around us, we realized we were far from land and were surrounded by big boats, in imminent danger of being cut in two by them at any moment. We finally decided to anchor and made up our minds that we had to stay there for the night. I remember Aunt Gladys walking around the deck, her sealskin coat absolutely white with fog.

There was nothing to eat on board, of course. Little Doris Rankin, who was with us, was then about eight years old. She and I were amusing ourselves by hanging pieces of string with pins on them over the side of the boat, and suddenly one of us caught a fish. No one in the party could believe that the first fish was caught without any bait. We soon had enough fish to supply supper for everybody, and Mrs. Rankin cooked them very beautifully over an oil stove in the little galley. Doris was wrapped up in a rug and put to sleep on a bench and I was put to sleep near her.

Nothing else happened that night, and in the morning when the fog lifted, we found we were very close to a little island. My uncle and some of the men went off in a boat and came back with milk, eggs and butter. We had a wonderful breakfast and went on our way to Bangor, where we found the house had been sold out the evening before. It had been a wonderful night, with the battleships in, and the house, as we had expected, had been very splendid. No one had known where we were and there had been a brilliant, though restless audience facing the prospect of no performance. The people were so discouraged at our failure to appear that naturally the next night no one came to see us.

After that tour closed I joined Mummum, who had gone to live with my uncle, John Drew, at the Sherman Square Hotel in New York City. There is a terribly trite word but I don't know any other to use to express what happened then; suddenly I found myself a pawn—a very unimportant thing that gets moved around a lot. I did nothing at all because of my own planning or thinking. I did what I was told. Like the pawn, I was picked up from that Canadian tour, moved by train with Uncle Sidney and Aunt Gladys and dropped at the Sherman Square Hotel in New York, and told to ask for my Uncle Jack's apartment. There I went and found Mummum.

She had a room and I was given a sort of room, the first "friar's cell." It was little and dark, the sort of room I had in my own first apartment where Jack used to come and sleep. Very often there are "friar's cells" in apartments, even in houses. At the Sherman Square Hotel I was in the "friar's cell," next to Mummum.

Of course I was a little bit bewildered. Mummum had been the pivot of the entire family and now something had happened and all the values were different. There was no explanation, and it would never have occurred to me to ask for one.

Even today I cannot tell why all this came about. It is a characteristic of my family that we never talked intimately to each other about the important things—never. Today I think that this is rather tragic.

But at fifteen I did what I was told to do and quite happily. The new surroundings, the changes put me in a state of mind that was not quite a daze—a sort of suspended animation.

Mummum was still there, very reticent, a person of absolutely enormous dignity and silences. She had a comfortable room and she was Mrs. John Drew, Uncle Jack's mother. But it was Uncle Jack's apartment, not her house. He was then the prosperous member of the family, a leading man at Daly's.

Uncle Jack was reticent, too—not so much as his mother

except about personal things, which he never discussed at
all. How can you put into words impressions in those early
days of someone known so well? I didn't, as a child, sit back
and say, "My, he is distinguished!" Of course he was.

The Sherman Square Hotel was at Seventy-first and
Broadway and is still there. It was an apartment hotel, just
a good, well-built hotel. Every morning I used to leave it
and go trudging from agency to agency, looking for a job.
This, too, had been decided for me and, naturally, I did not
think of protesting. Put away (though not forgotten for a
long while) were the dreams of living a life of music and
of a concert career. Every day I tried to find a job in the
theater and I could not.

Always the answers were the same, "Nothing today!"—
sometimes with a pleasant smile, sometimes with a frown.
Apparently belonging to a well-known theater family is a
handicap rather than a help. I have never known why this
is, but all my children have found it so and I certainly did.

Mummum was unhappy at being dependent for the first
time in her life, although it was on her own son, and she
was bewildered by my not getting a job—all very tragic for
her because she had been such a commanding person with
everyone's life in her hands for so many years. But instead
of drooping, her back seemed to get straighter and straighter
as she gazed out over the sinister rooftops of New York.
I felt so sad because I couldn't help. It was the beginning
of a long life of wondering where money was and where it
went after one found it.

This was during my fifteenth year. Although I felt very
grown up, I was still terribly young, young by the standards

of any era. Perhaps the convent was partly responsible for this, but more of it was due to the fact that in our family children were supposed not only to be seen and not heard but to be practically idiotic.

Day after day I kept on going to the agencies and various offices and came home without the faintest sign of an engagement or even a hope of one. I never did get an engagement in this way, although I went out early in the morning and spent the entire day sitting around, waiting for nothing. I do not think I shall ever forget the offices of Mrs. Fernandez, and Simmons and Brown; I spent so many hours waiting in them! No smallest chance was offered me —not even a stock engagement!

Thus passed the time from September to January, a time of continual searching and of great discouragement. The peculiar rumble of the old cable cars seemed to sing of my daily search for nothing, as time and again I returned home without a job and burning up with embarrassment over the thought of living on other people. I was not terrible to look at then, and certainly had youth in my favor and a name, and yet I remained at large.

Richard Harding Davis and a group of his friends used to come to see Uncle Jack. Charles Dana Gibson was one of them and John Fox and Bobby Russell and James Barnes and Arthur Leigh, who became Lord Leigh and gave Chequers to be the residence of the British Prime Minister. (Long afterward all of them were ushers at Dick Davis's wedding to Cecil Clark at which I was the only bridesmaid.)

I used to beg Dick Davis to talk about London because I had never gotten London out of my system since I was six years old. I had always wanted to go back. Sometimes I absolutely longed to go.

Dick Davis thought I ought to have some diversion and meet people of my own age. It was Dick who persuaded Uncle Jack to let me go to Dana Gibson's wedding to Irene Langhorne. Dick's sister Nora and I traveled to Richmond in a drawing room. It was an enormous wedding at the Jefferson Hotel in Richmond. This was where I first knew Nancy Langhorne. I thought then that she was a most attractive and brilliant girl, and I was not surprised when, after she married Waldorf Astor, she went on to the career that is history.

This was Uncle Jack's third year under the management of Charles Frohman, who had begun to institute the star system in the American theater with Uncle Jack his first star. Maude Adams, then Uncle Jack's leading lady, became Mr. Frohman's second star three years later in *The Little Minister*. Before going to Mr. Frohman Uncle Jack had been for years leading man of the Augustin Daly company, which had sometimes come to Philadelphia, but as I was in the convent during those years, I had seen only one of their plays, an unsuccessful one by Tennyson, called *The Foresters* in which Uncle Jack played Robin Hood. I've always been sorry that I never saw him as Petruchio, one of his greatest successes.

I still couldn't get a job, and so Uncle Jack finally arranged with Mr. Frohman that I should have some understudying chores and a little tray carrying in his company.

What I did then and during all my three years with Uncle Jack was done in order to eat. I had not stopped hurting

about not being a pianist. I went on the stage because I did
not know how to do anything but act—and I did not know
how to do that. I had not become an ambitious actress.
In fact I never have.

While I was carrying trays in Uncle Jack's play, I went
to a Yale prom with Cecil Clark's brother Bruce and a
girl named Ethel Gardner from Boston. I bought a ready-
made black satin skirt and made my black chiffon waist
myself. Fortunately I had been taught to sew in the convent
—not very well but needs must. Bruce's mother, a perfectly
delightful person, came on from Chicago to chaperone us.

Of course this was in the days when no young girl ever
went anywhere without an older woman as chaperone.
There was no such thing as boys and girls going out together
on "dates"—in fact the word had not yet been invented.
The only places where I saw young men were in my
friends' houses, at dinners or at other parties.

My going on such excursions as to the Yale Prom did not
disrupt the play, but there was always a mild protest from
Uncle Jack before he gave me permission.

He'd say, "Death!"—he never used any stronger oath than
that although sometimes he would say, "Death and the
young sculptor!"—which must have been part of a quotation
I have never been able to identify—"You can't do that. You
can't leave the play," and then he'd let me go.

At the Lyceum Theatre where Sothern was playing
Rudolf Rassendyll in *The Prisoner of Zenda,* they had
Thursday matinees, and as Uncle Jack played matinees on
Wednesday, I could go almost every week to see Sothern.
I had a crush on him; I bought his picture and dreamed

about Rudolf Rassendyll just as romantically as any school-girl. I think that Dick Davis thought I ought to meet Sothern. At any rate, he arranged a lunch at Delmonico's at which I sat next to what I thought was a middle-aged gentleman—he was probably between thirty and thirty-five —who was very nice to me. He turned out to be Mr. Sothern, but he was *not* Rudolf Rassendyll, and I recovered from my crush, although I still loved to go back on Thursday afternoons, whenever I could, to Ruritania.

When my cousin Louise Drew went abroad to go to school at Versailles, Aunt Dodo, her mother, went to live in Paris to be near her. They took Mummum with them and I left the Sherman Square Hotel and went to live in Mrs. Wilson's boardinghouse on Thirty-sixth Street. It was one of a row of brownstone houses. On top of the newel post in the front hall was the statue of a Nubian slave holding up a shaded gas lamp that was always turned down very low when we came in from the theater at night.

I had a hall bedroom and three meals a day for $9 a week, so that even on the $30 a week that I was earning, I could pay for my clothes and hope to save against the lean and hungry summer and toward the realization of my dream of going back to London.

Maude Adams was living at Mrs. Wilson's with her mother and that is how Uncle Jack heard about it and knew it would be a nice place for me to stay. At that time I did not know Maude at all and we saw very little of her at the boardinghouse. Mrs. Wilson was a dressmaker and made the loveliest of clothes. She always made Maude's dresses, and later she was to make all of my costumes for *Captain*

Jinks. There was no place in her house in which to receive a man caller or, for that matter, a caller of any kind, but sometimes she would let us use the front parlor where she did her fittings.

One night Ida Conquest, another actress who was also living at Mrs. Wilson's, came down to dinner in full evening dress. We all said, "Where are you going?"

"Nowhere," she said haughtily. "I always dress for dinner," which caused a mild hysteria. It appeared she was going to have a visitor.

This became another of the family wheezes.

My cousin Georgie Mendum, who had come to New York to go on the stage, also lived at Mrs. Wilson's. She was an enchanting person. One Saturday we got a little money, and I thought it would be wonderful to have something hot after the theater so I went around the corner to a lunch counter called Minks on Sixth Avenue. It was a place with a counter like a horseshoe—no table—and everybody was sitting, busily eating. Timidly I whispered to the waiter, "I would like two club sandwiches to take home."

He turned around and screamed, "Two clubs going out." Every eye in the place turned and gave me a searching look. I was so frightened I wanted to die.

Georgie stayed in the theater for a long time. She was awfully good. She was a terrific reader but didn't care much about anything that was less than two or three thousand years old. She had a really fabulous knowledge of the church fathers and the early church.

In those days no actor thought of playing a whole season in New York. It was the custom to play there for three months or so and for the rest of the season in other cities, which were regarded of equal importance. Uncle Jack, like Irving, Terry, Bernhardt and Duse when they came to this country, followed this custom, and so presently *The Bauble Shop* in which I had been carrying trays, was about to go on tour.

Elsie de Wolfe, who had been playing the part of Lady Kate Fennell, did not want to leave New York and, although I was barely sixteen and the author, Henry Arthur Jones, had described Lady Kate Fennell in the program as "A Woman of the World, of 45," some maniac suggested that I be given a trial in the part. So one Wednesday afternoon, wearing Miss de Wolfe's beautiful Paquin clothes and feeling very terrified and perhaps a little ridiculous, I played the part. When they found that I didn't actually fall on my face they let me have the part when they went on tour, and I wore those Paquin clothes. Miss de Wolfe was very indignant that her name was still on the program with such an inadequate person taking her place on that matinee afternoon. It was not of sufficient importance, my appearing, to have the program changed.

Thus it was that I traveled with my uncle, receiving a very small salary, of course, and living in the cheapest of hotels and boardinghouses. Uncle Jack was very kind to me and I occasionally met some of his friends when I went to see him. As I remember, I enjoyed myself very much, although I never had any clothes to wear which I really liked.

In Chicago I remember that one notice referred to me as "an opalescent dream named Ethel Barrymore that came on and played Lady Kate." I hadn't the faintest idea what that word meant and had to ask Uncle Jack. I was delighted to find it meant something pleasant.

On that tour I began to know the other cities of America and to form, with the people who lived in them, friendships that have lasted all my life.

In Boston, even before I came to know people there, the city itself fascinated me—the Common and the Public Gardens in the very heart of the city were to me always thrilling; I loved Beacon Street, too, and Mount Vernon Street and most of all the eighteenth-century charm of Louisburg Square, that always seemed to have, like the modern Bostonians, a kind of tincture of the cavalier blended with its puritanism.

Through Dick Davis I knew Jack and Sally Fairchild. Long afterward it was from the Jack Fairchild house that I was married. It was on later visits that I came to know the Sears and the Thayers and to see Mrs. Jack Gardner's wonderful garden inside her house in Fenway Park. What an extraordinary woman she was—what a character!

But on my first visit I began to go to hear the Boston Symphony, one of the greatest of all orchestras, and I have always gone to hear it whenever I could. In those great days Nikisch was conductor and Kneisel was concert master, and also playing were Timothée and Joseph Adamowski and Charles Loeffler, who were to be the other members of the famous Kneisel Quartet. The symphony was founded by Colonel Higginson with whose son Alex I went to a Harvard Class Day. A little while ago, just before she died, I went with Mrs. Higginson to hear Koussevitzky and she was still thinking of the symphony as "her" orchestra.

In New York Uncle Jack had taken me to a wedding where I met a girl named Dora Harris, and when I was in Philadelphia at Mrs. Langdon's boardinghouse, Dora sent me a note to say that she was staying with a school friend, Frances McCullough, and that Frances and her parents would be very happy if I would come to Sunday tea. So I went to their house in Rittenhouse Square, where the Barclay Hotel is today, and this began a friendship that has lasted to this minute.

I remember that I had only a blue serge cape and that the wind used to blow through it. Frances and Dora kept telling me I ought to have a coat and kept asking me why I didn't get one. I didn't want to tell them that I didn't have money with which to buy one. I said, "Next year I am going to get a white serge suit; in winter it will be warm because it is serge, and in summer it will be cool because it is white."

I did get the white suit, but I had forgotten about the cleaning bills. I paid for it over and over.

Frances was stage-struck. She never missed any play that came to Philadelphia and had scrapbooks full of clippings. All her life she adored the theater. I've never known anybody so crazy about it.

She married Mitchell Rosengarten when he was going to the Spanish-American War. He had gone to the University of Pennsylvania and his brother Harold to Princeton. They both played on the football teams and when Penn and Princeton met, they just about murdered each other. I think Mitchell Rosengarten was one of the most attractive, charming, ugly men I ever knew. He and Fran had a lovely daughter, Peggy. She looked like a daffodil, a most exquisite creature. When people dropped in late in the afternoon, Fran would turn languidly to Peggy and say, "Peg, mix," and Peg, about ten years old, would produce a shaker of cocktails.

The first time Uncle Jack heard this, he was very startled, but the phrase became another of the family wheezes.

Philadelphia has always seemed to me to have an atmosphere of greatness, perhaps because of Benjamin Franklin, the Continental Congress and the Declaration of Independence. And Philadelphia people always gave one the impression of permanence, of having been there for a long, long time—as of course they have. It took far more than three generations to become an old family in Philadelphia, although three appear to be plenty long enough in most other cities.

What I remember best about going to balls in those days were the lovely cotillions. As clearly as if I had seen it yesterday, I remember one beautiful figure, a man with two ribbons for reins driving four lovely girls, Mazie and Susie Sturgis, Helen Saunders, and Daisy Godfrey. Cotillions, I realize now, provided a wonderful opportunity to see beauty in a way which is not possible in the modern, crowded ballroom.

It was when I was on tour with Uncle Jack that I went to a Hunt Ball in Baltimore. All the men were in pink coats, and everything was very grand until a man who was a little tight began pursuing me. He frightened me so that without even getting a coat I ran out into the snow and all the way back to the Stafford Hotel. It was idiotic, of course, but it's what I did.

In Washington Uncle Jack took me to a lunch at the British Embassy. Afterward the whole party went out for a drive in Sam Holland's four-in-hand. The First Secretary of the Embassy, Bax Ironside, sat beside me. He said, "You live in Washington?"

I said, "No, I'm just here for this week."

"Oh, just a week? Have you come to stay with anyone?"

I said, "No, I'm playing here."

He said, "Playing? Playing what?"

I said, "I am acting here."

He said, "Acting? Does it amuse you?"

In Washington I knew Helen and Alice Hay, daughters of Mr. John Hay, who was later Ambassador to the Court of St. James's and Secretary of State. I was always thrilled by the fact that as a young man Mr. Hay had been Abraham Lincoln's private secretary. Knowing him seemed to bring me impressively close to Lincoln himself. The attic of the Hay house in Lafayette Square had been turned over to Helen and Alice as a playroom. They had decorated it with Toulouse-Lautrec posters, and they had their piano and guitars there. They would be seeing their friends up there while more important things were happening downstairs. Their friendship meant much to me then and always.

In Cincinnati I knew the Longworths, Nicholas and his mother and his sister Mrs. Wallingford. I remember being taken to a ballgame there by Nick and Julius Fleischmann. Nick was one of the best amateur violinists I have ever known and a perfectly charming creature. I always loved him.

In Milwaukee on that first tour I very nearly lost my life.

On Saturday night I had left a call to be wakened in time
to go to seven o'clock mass, as we were leaving early for
Chicago. As always I read until quite late and when I stood
up in bed to turn out the gaslight, hanging from the center
of the ceiling, something was wrong with the fixture so that
instead of just turning off the gas, I turned it on again.
In the morning when they couldn't wake me, they found
me unconscious in a room full of gas. They got me resus-
citated, not in time for mass but in time to go, very sickly,
with the rest of the company to Chicago.

When we were in Chicago Mrs. Arthur Caton (later
Mrs. Marshall Field) was giving a ball. Uncle Jack thought
I was too young to go to a grown-up party, but Mrs. Caton
—Aunt Delia—and her niece and nephew, Katharine and
Spencer Eddy, persuaded him to let me go. That was a sort
of Chicago debut for me.

I was to have many friends there, Medill McCormick and
his wife Ruth Hanna; Florence and Minna Fields, whose
mother married Thomas Nelson Page; Ru Carpenter; Nancy
Coleman; and many, many others. Some of the earliest of
those friendships were with the writers and artists like
Finley Peter Dunne, George Ade, John McCutcheon and
others who were just beginning—or hadn't yet begun—to
make their mark.

I remember that once Hal Rhodes and Herbert Stone
were discussing my voice right in front of me and Herbert,
who was being very knowing, said: "I think it's because of
all the generations of her people on the stage who had to
talk in unnatural voices."

I said indignantly: "None of them ever talked in an unnatural voice at all!"

That was one part of this profession of mine in which I was very fortunate. I came from people who spoke well, from a family where purity of speech was a matter of course, where there was no such thing as a provincial accent. If I brought a provincialism home from school, eyebrows were raised so far that they disappeared into that thick Drew hair, and that particular provincialism would never be uttered again. In running her stock company at the Arch Street Theatre, Mummum had absolutely no patience, no tolerance whatever, for slipshod speech. At home she and everyone else spoke well. Nothing was ever said about it. It was just done.

I loved St. Louis then as I have loved it ever since. Even then it was an old, mellow, gracious city, cultured, sophisticated, civilized and—above all—relaxed. And it has imperturbably refused to allow a change-worshiping century to change it in any of these respects. It already had an interesting group of literary people like Sara Teasdale and Orrick Johns and William Reedy who published *Reedy's Mirror,* in which so many writers who were later to be famous were being given their first chance at print. Zoë Akins was there, too—and a young man, rather on the fringe of this group, named T. S. Eliot.

There were other interesting groups besides the literary one—the old French and the Germans, still keeping a little apart from each other and from the Americans, and I found friends in all of them—friends like the Busches, the Lamberts and Dwight and Helen Davis, givers of the Davis tennis cup. And in St. Louis, long before Irvin Cobb began writing stories about an imaginary one, I knew a real Judge Priest, a perfectly charming person.

Denver always seemed to me to be somehow conscious of the fact that it was a mile high and blown by clean winds. I never felt that it changed very much—but I saw many changes in the beautiful place a few miles away that was Colorado Springs. When I first knew it, some friends of mine, the Baldwins, had built a white marble house, a little trianon, that was an astonishing thing to come upon suddenly, standing in splendid royalty in the middle of a desert long before the city grew up about it and the great broadmoor Hotel was built just beyond it.

Salt Lake City was beautiful, with the lovely poplar trees that Brigham Young had planted. I have always admired his genius and his terrific courage—a truly great man.

We played four performances there, in the wonderful theater the Mormons built. On Thursday night the two lower boxes, on each side of the stage, were occupied by the oldest wives of Heber Smith, the head of the Mormon Church. On Friday night the middle-aged wives were there; at the Saturday matinee, millions of children, and on Saturday evening, the youngest wives.

The theater was beautiful, a very "theater" theater with an atmosphere that reminded me of the Arch Street Theatre. It had a sloping stage, like the English stages—almost the last one left in America, I think, although I remember coming unexpectedly on another one, in a New Orleans theater I hadn't played before, and running almost down to the footlights.

Years after that first tour with Uncle Jack I played in the old Salt Lake City theater, just before it was torn down to make room for a telephone building.

San Francisco seemed to me then and has seemed to me ever since the most exciting of American cities. There was —and still is—in it some of the exuberant aliveness of its gold rush days, and yet it was already a civilized, sophisticated, cultured city, with a magnificent symphony orchestra and a group of such writers as Frank Norris, Ambrose Bierce, Jack London, Gertrude Atherton, Charles and Kathleen Norris and many others.

Then and afterward I knew them all. I always thought that Ambrose Bierce was a truly great writer, and that he would have been still greater if he had lived out his life instead of going to Mexico on that tragically unimportant job of reporting the Villa incident. There are some terrific stories in his *Soldiers and Civilians*.

In San Francisco Uncle Jack had some enchanting friends. These were the Tobins—the Tobini, we called them. Richard Tobin was a wonderfully good polo player and also a wonderful violinist, so good that he would bring three members of the San Francisco orchestra down to his house at Burlingame, and he would play second violin in the quartet.

When I first stayed with the Tobins at Burlingame, it was real country, but Mr. William Crocker and the Carolans were building great houses, surrounded by beautiful gardens, colossal palazzos, with mantelpieces, doors, panelings, even whole rooms, brought from England and Italy.

There was never time enough when I was on tour with

Uncle Jack for me to do the things I wanted to do. There were people to see, other matinees to go to, recitals, concerts —the symphonies were growing—drives to take, and in between and always, reading, reading, reading, *eating* books as I had begun to eat them in Mummum's library whenever I came home from the convent, and as I have been doing to this day.

I was very eager. I loved seeing America and I wanted to see it all. And it was a wonderful time to begin seeing America—just at the end of an era in which changes had been gentle and slow, just at the beginning of the changes that were to be so tremendous and so fiercely swift.

I knew Euclid Avenue in Cleveland and Delaware Avenue in Buffalo before the proud, old houses under the arching elms had become grim rooming houses, black with soot. And I knew cities like Dayton where houses that were old and gracious then have somehow managed to survive unchanged, and like Toledo where some of the same old, lovely houses still look out over their wide lawns to the river. I saw Detroit when it was still a small city, not so very different from places like Jackson and Kalamazoo—the celery was good in Kalamazoo and so was the audience. Audiences were —and are—always good in one-night towns where they are composed so largely of people who really want to see the play and have only this one chance to see it. One of these audiences in Little Rock, Arkansas, was the best I ever played to. I remember it that way because they were so eager to be pleased. When an audience is like that, they help you so; you know they are with you and you don't have that extra drain on your energy to keep them from coughing or moving about in their seats. One-night stands are the best audiences in America. I never minded the physical effort of traveling, never even thought about it.

That first tour was the beginning of a lifetime of playing all the large cities in America and most of the little ones. In every one of them I found friends.

Often and often I have been asked how, when I was a young, shy girl staying in cities I had never seen before, I came to know so many people. The only answer I have ever found for that question is, I haven't the faintest idea. All of a sudden I just knew people and they were my friends.

Perhaps one reason was that I was always interested in everything—in music, books, painting, politics, baseball and —above all—in people.

During these years I saw nothing of my father and almost nothing of Lionel and Jack. Jack was in school and Lionel was already on the stage. He played briefly with Mummum and Uncle Googan in *The Rivals* and then with McKee Rankin, Aunt Gladys's father. His part in Mr. Rankin's production of *Magda* was the same one that Jack first played when, a little later, he also went on the stage in Mr. Rankin's company.

It was the part of a young officer and Jack's uniform inspired Amy Leslie, the drama critic of the Chicago *News*, to write: "Jack Barrymore looked as if he had been dressed up and forgotten."

Jack always loved to tell this story.

Lionel went on playing in *Arizona* and other plays.

It was sad that we didn't see each other.

It was during my first tour with Uncle Jack that I got to

know Maude Adams a little. One night in Springfield, Massachusetts, we had supper of crackers and milk together after the theater, and sat and talked. I thought this evening was wonderful. I remember how Dick Davis adored her, as all of her friends did, and how later when we were playing New Haven we went to a tea given by an undergraduate in his rooms and she delighted all the boys by singing for them. For two or three years she was perfectly charming and gay, and then she began to be the original "I want-to-be-alone" woman. On long journeys all the way across the country, she would never come out of her berth, and it was very rarely that anybody saw her off the stage. I never knew whether this was Mr. Frohman's idea or her own. I have always had a great feeling for her, although I never knew her any better. She was a rare spirit, and I am glad I touched her even lightly.

All the time I was on tour with Uncle Jack I lived in the cheapest boardinghouse rooms I could find, and I found them for myself. In every theater a notice would be posted on the call board a day or two before we were to move on to the next town listing the available accommodations there, starting with the most expensive hotel and going on down to the cheapest boardinghouses, which were the ones that interested me.

Nobody paid any attention to me. Our elders were helping out those Barrymore children to the extent of seeing that we ate. Except for that I didn't get anything from Uncle Googan, and when I went on tour with Uncle Jack I had my salary—though small—and was supposed to live on it, and I did, without any advice or supervision from anybody.

Even then the only clothes I had were my winter and summer convent uniforms. I bought a piece of French-blue velvet and made a sort of collar of it which I wore on my black serge school dresses so they wouldn't look so uniformy. I was wearing it when I had my picture taken with Maude Adams in Springfield, Massachusetts.

I spent two Christmases in a hall bedroom in Pittsburgh —I never had any real Christmases after Mummum's house until I had children and there was reason for a tree. There was always a Christmas matinee until I was on my own and refused to play them any more. They were never profitable. Playing them was just an old, bad established custom.

Once when we were in Boston I stayed at the Langham Hotel where, instead of a hall bedroom, I had a sitting room, bedroom and bath and three meals a day, all for $15 a week! This was when I was playing in *Rosemary* and was finished after the second act so that I could leave at ten o'clock. I always walked home from the theater and part of the way to the hotel led through a very brightly lighted district where everybody was cheerful and friendly. Apparently after the first few nights they got to know my face, and they'd say, "Hello, dearie, how are you tonight?"

I thought they were all perfectly charming. It was years later I discovered I had been walking through the red-light district, but I have never changed my mind about how friendly and nice they were.

Sometimes during the summers of those years I would spend a few weeks in Marion, Massachusetts, where I stayed with the Davises or the Clarks, and occasionally I would stay for a few days at Uncle Jack's at Easthampton, but most of the time I spent at Mrs. Wilson's boardinghouse and most of it I spent reading.

I read all of Dumas and all of Dickens and I have never stopped reading them. I still read and reread *Twenty Years After* and *The Vicomte de Bragelonne* over and over. I think Porthos' will is one of the best chapters in literature and I cry every time I read it. I love the Valois series, too, and I still enjoy reading about Chicot, the jester, on his mission from Henry III to Henry of Navarre. Chicot seems to me to be one of the great characters in fiction—and not actually fiction either for he was a real person, a nobleman who chose to be a jester for Henry III.

I still read at least two Dickens books every year. *David Copperfield* is my favorite—I love the people in it, but I like *Pickwick Papers,* too. Henry Irving played Jingle fifty years before I saw him and whenever I read *Pickwick* Mr. Jingle seems to look like Irving. The Cruikshank drawings really do look like him. It was in this play that Sir Henry made his first impression—one English paper referred to "an arresting young man, Henry Irving, as Jingle."

I read Poe, too, and I still think that "The Gold Bug" and "The Murders in the Rue Morgue" are the best of all the classic detective stories. Poe's own tragic story always fascinated me. There was no happiness for him anywhere. I have always thought that he, too, was born under a dark star.

I read and loved all of Frank Stockton's stories, and I am sorry for the people who do not know them. If I were a publisher, the first book I would print would be a new edition of *The Bee Man of Orne.*

And there were some stories, too, by a new writer named Rudyard Kipling. I loved them as I kept on loving everything that Kipling wrote. I feel the same way toward the people who think it isn't intellectual to read him as I do toward the people who don't like Beethoven.

And I feel the same way about the people who make fun of *Little Lord Fauntleroy* without ever having read it. I still read it every year and still cry. I think that Mrs. Burnett had a spark of genius; nothing less than that it seems to me could have written not only *Little Lord Fauntleroy* but books so amazingly different from it and from each other as *That Lass o' Lowrie's* and *T. Tembarom*. I went through a period when I was terrifically fascinated by Turgeniev. Perhaps it was an anti-Russian period—Turgeniev is so utterly unlike all other Russians. I had a Hardy period, too, when I thought Tess was wonderful, and for some reason I cannot now understand actually enjoyed the depressing *Jude the Obscure*. I also had a wonderful time with *Diana of the Crossways*, and *The Ordeal of Richard Feverel*, but except for some of his poems, I can't read Meredith now.

The same thing has happened with other writers and other books. Frances McCullough and Dora Harris and I, unbeknown to each other, all read and loved *Myra of the Pines*, by Herman Knickerbocker Vielé. It was a short book; we thought it full of humor and charm and could quote from it word for word. Once when Frances was staying at Dora's in New York we all went to a party and met the author, who was overwhelmed and slightly alarmed by three girls who knew his book by heart. But just the other day I got hold of the book again and found it perfectly impossible to read.

My tastes then, and since, were very, very catholic. I knew *Alice in Wonderland* almost by heart and have never stopped loving it. Years afterward when I was staying with Virginia Jacklin at Woodside and she showed me her first edition of *Alice* I said, "I could cut your throat!" And I almost meant it.

I knew and still know Edward Lear practically by heart. Nobody can start a Lear limerick that I can't finish.

Peter Dunne's stories about Mr. Dooley were making everybody laugh and making many people think. I have always thought that he was a writer of enormous importance. Some of the things he wrote were brought up in the House of Commons. What Mr. Dooley would be saying to Mr. Hennessey about some people in the public eye if Peter Dunne were alive today!

Of course I loved Stevenson. Something about his writing always made me cry, especially *A Child's Garden of Verses,* so lovely, so touching, all of them, but most of all "In winter I get up at night"—what a heartbreaker! I used to make up tunes for those verses and sing them to myself.

Years later I was to own all of N. C. Wyeth's original illustrations for *Kidnapped* and *David Balfour,* some of the most beautiful paintings, I think, that he ever made.

Jack was crazy about *The Master of Ballantrae* and always wanted it made into a play or movie for him.

There were so many books that I loved, by such quite unlike authors—everything of Henry James—I loved his sentences that lasted for three pages—and, more exciting to me then and since, everything of his brother William's, too. I had a terrific "thing" about William James; I remember going to his house in Cambridge long after his death and sitting in his chair, a queer sort of rocking chair, and having a strange feeling of his presence in the room.

And at the same time I was reading Henry and William James I was loving *The Story of an African Farm,* by Olive Schreiner, and *Friendship* and *Under Two Flags,* by Ouida, and those delightfully imaginative Ruritania books, *The Prisoner of Zenda,* and *Rupert of Hentzau,* by Anthony Hope, whom I was later to know in London. It was Anthony who invented the whole idea of an imaginary modern European kingdom that so many later writers have imitated. I have always resented those imitations. Anthony also invented another fiction form in *The Dolly Dialogues,* which he wrote when he was quite young.

I had begun to worship Mark Twain, and since I have been writing this book I have often thought of what he once wrote—"I find that the farther I go back the better I remember things, whether they happened or not." And in times like these it is rather comforting to think how long ago Mark Twain wrote, "We have idiots and Congressmen —but I repeat myself!"

It was some time after those days and nights at Mrs. Wilson's and on tour that I began to read and love poetry, but I have never stopped reading it and loving it. I am an absolute lunatic about William Blake. I have a special love for Keats and Shelley, for some of Francis Thompson, for some of John Donne, for all of Walt Whitman, for all of Shakespeare, not only the plays but the sonnets. But I love all poetry except for the very modern kind. I don't know what that means.

Among my favorite reading Matthew, Mark, Luke and John also have a special place.

After three years with Uncle Jack I had my first good part with him in a play called *Rosemary* in which Maude Adams was the leading lady. There was a small maid's part that was very effective and this fell to me. The public was kind and the papers were even kinder, and I felt myself beginning— at last!

But the great dream of my life was still to go to London. I had always loved the thought of it and had never been able to get it out of my mind. I saw no hopes for many years of getting there but this did not weaken my determination, someday, in some way, to get to London.

I was very romantic at this time and had matinee crushes. My crush was William Gillette, who was playing in *Secret Service*. Fortunately for my young heart, he had matinees on the days we didn't, and thus I was able to go every Thursday and rapturously admire him. I had his photograph— which I had bought—and hoped that someday I would have the thrill of meeting him, feeling just as romantic about him as I had felt long before about Rudolf Rassendyll.

After the New York run of *Rosemary*, I went on tour with Uncle Jack. We had reached St. Louis and one night he called me to his dressing room and said: "I have just had a most extraordinary telegram from C. F. about you."

He handed it to me and I read:

WOULD ETHEL LIKE TO GO TO LONDON WITH GILLETTE
IN SECRET SERVICE?

EMPIRE THEATRE

BROADWAY and 40th STREET

(ERECTED AND OWNED BY FRANK W. SANGER AND AL. HAYMAN.)

CHARLES FROHMAN, RICH & HARRIS, ... LESSEES

CHARLES FROHMAN . . . . MANAGER

Evenings at 8.20.   Matinees Wednesday and Saturday.

EXTRA MATINEE ELECTION DAY, NOV 3.

FIFTH SEASON OF THIS THEATRE.

AND FIFTH SEASON OF

MR. JOHN DREW,

Under the management of CHARLES FROHMAN,

Presenting, for the first time in this country, a play, in four acts, entitled

ROSEMARY.

"That's for remembrance."

By LOUIS N. PARKER and MURRAY CARSON.

SIR JASPER THORNDYKE..JOHN DREW
PROFESSOR JOGRAM. ....DANIEL HARKINS
CAPTAIN CRUICKSHANK, R. N................ ....HARRY HARWOOD
WILLIAM WESTWOOD. .. ..ARTHUR BYRON
GEORGE MINIFIE.......................................GRAHAME HENDERSON
ABRAHAM.................... ....FRANK E. LAMB
MRS. CRUICKSHANK...Mrs. ANNIE ADAMS
MRS. MINIFIE...Mrs. DELOSS KING
PRISCILLA.................... ....ETHEL BARRYMORE
DOROTHY CRUICKSHANK ....MAUDE ADAMS

Programme continued on second page following.

Why I didn't drop dead, I do not know. This great news was almost too much for me. My uncle was bewildered at my excitement and looked at me curiously.

"Do you really want to go?" he asked.

I said, "More than anything in the world."

Uncle Jack said, "Death! What nonsense!" But after he saw how I felt he said, "Very well, you can go if you want to so much. We'll find someone to replace you."

As soon as they did, I was on the train to New York and soon after that, with a small bag that carried everything I owned, I was given my ticket and told to go to the boat for the journey to wonderful London with wonderful Gillette.

My father, whom I had not seen for several years, heard about my leaving and promised to come down to the dock to see me off. As he was a great friend of Gillette, he said he would introduce me to him, but knowing his genius for irresponsibility, I wasn't too disappointed when he didn't turn up. As the boat drew away from the pier, I was standing on the deck with Harry Woodruff, a young actor in the company whom I just knew, when toward us walked the tall figure who was the dream of my life at the moment.

I whispered to Harry, "I don't know him."

"Oh!" he said, "I'll introduce you."

Gillette bowed over my hand and I thought, "Oh, no! This isn't what I meant at all!"

And it wasn't.

Getting off the train at Waterloo Station I immediately felt I'd come home. The wooden pavements, wet with that lovely rain, smelled like heaven. I had no idea I'd been missing it so much.

This was the summer of Queen Victoria's Diamond Jubilee, celebrating the sixtieth anniversary of her coronation. I saw the parade from someone's house in Piccadilly. It was a terrific spectacle, more magnificent, I think, than any of the coronation parades that followed it. I shall never forget the Indian princes, dripping from chin to waist with fabulous jewels, unbelievable strings of pearls, diamonds and rubies.

I found lodgings in Chapel Street. I was much too shy to present any of the letters Sally Fairchild had given me to the Sidney Webbs and Bernard Shaw and many other Fabians, all of whom I met quite painlessly later on, but some of the people to whom Dick Davis had written looked me up and I began at once to go about with them and have good times.

As all the cast, except for me, had been in the play in New York, there were only a few rehearsals before we opened. My part in *Secret Service* was very small; I had been engaged primarily as an understudy. In those days understudying was not taken seriously, nor is it taken seriously today; it is more or less of a theory in the American theater that leading actors and actresses never get ill. And in reality we don't often miss a performance; it is a rare thing when a theater has to be closed because of illness.

But one night after the curtain had gone up and I was sitting on the stage in my nurse's costume, Odette Tyler, whom I was understudying in an ingénue part, fainted just before she was to make her entrance. The curtain had to come down and I heard shouts for me to come and play her part.

Unfortunately, I had never had a rehearsal, as understudies should have, and I was panic-stricken. "I can't," I said.

"You must!" they insisted.

I had seen the play over and over again because of my crush on Gillette, and I was perfectly familiar with it—at least, I thought I was. I rushed upstairs to Miss Tyler's room, tearing off my things as I went. Then I had immediately to put them on again when I found that Odette Tyler had been removed to the hospital—in her costume.

Dressed in my nurse's costume, I played the part as best I could. It was a great moment for me. The next day I got a dress and made an apparent success, so much so that I began receiving many letters and several of the critics came to see the play again and gave me real praise.

Miss Tyler continued ill and I continued in her part. I was sorry that she was ill and yet I was very happy that I was playing. It really looked as though everything had begun for me.

One morning I went to the theater for my mail and on the stage I saw some people rehearsing. They were rehearsing a new girl. They had cabled for her the day after Miss Tyler had been taken ill and, when she was ready the next day, I was sent to my old part of a few lines. It was my first heartbreak in the theater!

I don't remember the name of the actress who played my part; I don't believe she played again in anything. It was one of those strange incidents that happen in the theater which are never explained.

In spite of this disappointment, I clung to the idea that London was still London. I kept saying to myself, "I am

still in London, the place I want to be in more than anywhere else in the world." I determined that I would remain
in some way or other, no matter what happened. A great
many of the people who had been kind to me about my
performance in *Secret Service* were actor-managers of
prominence and they had all been very hearty in their praise
when I met them. "You must stay in London," they had said
to me, and it was natural that I should feel sure of getting
something to do. So I proceeded to go around among the
admiring throng who had praised me, but I had no practical
suggestions from them. In fact, I was not given a sign of
encouragement of getting anything of any kind to do.

Then one afternoon a hansom cab brought me a note.

(And let me digress to point out that in those days when
hansom cabs brought me my messages, I seemed to get them
just as quickly as if there had been telephones. What a
gracious life it was in those days of no telephones, no pass-
ports, no income taxes! Horse-and-buggy age? What was the
matter with the horse and buggy? What was the matter with
the hansom cab? Was there ever any lovelier way to travel,
any lovelier sound than the clop-clop of the horse's hoofs on
those wooden pavements in London? I feel so sorry for the
people who know only enough about those days to laugh at
them! My passion for hansom cabs came to be well known.
Once coming home on a boat, I met Peter Dunne who told
me that he had been in London. I said, "Why didn't you
come to see me?" And he said, "I forgot the number of
your cab!")

The note the cab brought me was from Cissie Loftus, saying that she was singing at an important house that night

and her accompanist was ill and would I play for her? We didn't have to get there till half past ten and I would be finished at the theater by then, so I said, "I'd love to." Afterward, as I was trying to get through the crowd to leave, Creighton Webb, a friend of Uncle Jack's, grabbed me and said:

"Ethel, you must come with me. The Duke of York wants me to present you to him."

I said, "Oh, no! I couldn't!"

He said, "You've got to."

I said, "What'll I do?"

He said, "Just curtsy. Come along behave yourself."

Suddenly I was looking at the bluest eyes I have ever seen and such a kindly smile, and he said: "Aren't you the little girl I saw in *Secret Service*?"

And I gasped, "Yes, sir."

He said, "You know I saw it again and you weren't playing the part. Why? I liked you so much better than the present girl."

I said, "Thank you, sir," and fled, very happy and blushing from head to foot.

As I ran I got a pleasant smile from the Duchess of York, and I often thought of it in later life when I saw her picture and heard stories of her when she became the great Queen Mary.

I wanted to stay in England after the play finished its run. People had been so nice to me. The people I saw most were "Uncle" Ben Webster, the actor; his wife, May Whitty, whom I called "Maisie Dreams"; Anthony Hope, the novelist; Didi and Alfred Littleton; and Etty and Willie

Grenfell. These I saw most and loved most. As I look back on it now, they were very wonderful to me—so wonderful in every way that I didn't realize at the time my good fortune in being allowed to know them so well and so intimately. I was still fairly young and took these honors as a matter of course. I suppose I liked them so much that I didn't see any reason why they should not like me. At any rate, they did like me, and all treated me as though I were truly one of them. Never for one moment did I ever feel that I belonged to a different world, which, of course, as a matter of fact, I did not.

The literary-theatrical group I found fascinating, though perhaps slightly irreverent in a happy way. I remember that there was one terrible evening when we were all at the Websters' to hear Laurence Irving read a short play he had written. He insisted on silence and began: "The play begins with a chorus of lepers."

There was an instant's silence and then dreadful laughter, Laurence leaving immediately in high dudgeon.

I was also great friends with quite a different group of people, Lady Lister-Kaye and Sir John and her sister the Duchess of Manchester and her beautiful young twin daughters and Kim, her son. Lady Lister-Kaye was very kind to me, and I would go very often to her house in Manchester Square. One of the people who was often there was Prince Francis of Teck whom they all called Frankie Teck. He used to talk a great deal about his sister, May, who was then the Duchess of York.

I also knew Sir George and Lady Lewis, whose daughter Elsie became a friend of mine. Sir George was one of the great solicitors of England; it was said of him that he knew the secrets of every great family in England. I used to go to wonderful dinners at their house. That was where I occasionally saw Sir Henry Irving. And Edie Craig, Ellen Terry's daughter, had a flat in the same building where the Websters lived and she took me to see Miss Terry.

One night at a big ball someone came up to me and said, "Lord Kitchener wants to dance with you."

I will never forget how frightened I was! He was like a man carved out of teak with green, terrifying eyes. He never spoke a single word but just kept looking down at me. When the dance was over, I felt as if I had been released from chains. In those days Englishmen didn't dance very well. They just hopped around. When I went to a ball, I always hoped that Jack Carter, the second secretary at the Embassy, would be there, and plenty of Hungarians and Austrians because they danced so well.

I had two dresses, one black and one white, which I found were quite enough for the highest and most exalted society. In London, somehow, people don't care who you are or what you have on; if they make up their minds they like you, they take you in and there you stay for all time.

I was really living in two worlds after *Secret Service* closed and I had no job. Unless I was asked out to dinner, I was often quite hungry though I found that if I didn't have any dinner in the offing, I could live on dates. Finally I realized how hopeless it all was; nothing was coming and I scarcely had money left to pay for my lodgings. I had to go and confess ignominiously to Uncle Jack, who was in London and about to sail to America, that I had failed, and I asked him if I could go back with him. He took it quite calmly and said:

"Oh, of course, of course. We'll see to it."

I was to bring back two beautiful dresses for the leading lady in Uncle Jack's play, *A Marriage of Convenience*. They were copies of authentic Louis XVI costumes, elaborate white satin and brocade. I was packing the dresses in the trunk that had been sent to my lodgings for the purpose and I was crying. I tried to keep any tears from falling on the dresses.

And a hansom cab stopped at the door with a note for me. It read: "Dear little Bullfinch: [That was the name Ellen Terry called me because she thought I looked like one.] I hear you're going back to America. Come down to the theatre tonight to say goodbye to Sir Henry and me. Ellen Terry."

So I washed my face and bathed my eyes and got into my black evening dress—I was going to a supper party at the Savoy, given by friends of Uncle Jack to say good-by to him —and went to the theater and up to Miss Terry's dressing room and she said: "So, you're going back to America! Go in and say good-by to Sir Henry."

I was, of course, terrified at the mere thought of facing him. But it was extremely nice of him to let me say good-by, so I went to Sir Henry's dressing room and he said, "So you want to go back to America?"

"No, Sir Henry," I said, "I don't, but I can't find anything to do."

And he said, "How would you like to stay here and be our little leading lady?"

"Oh, Sir Henry!" I could not say another word—I could not think of anything else.

"Well," he said, "you could play Annette in *The Bells* and there's a part in Laurence's play that I am going to do about Peter the Great. Now don't cry. Just go downstairs —Mr. Loveday has a contract all ready for you to sign. Run along."

Then I could not speak at all, and as he looked at me, he knew exactly the state I was in. I literally fell down the stairs to Mr. Loveday's office, and on the way I met Miss Terry. Again that radiant smile of hers as she said: "Are you happy?"

I threw my arms around her, exclaiming, "Oh! Oh!"

I have no remembrance of signing that contract. I only know that suddenly it was tucked away close to my fast-beating heart and I left the Lyceum Theatre, floating on a cloud to the farewell supper party.

Besides my aunt and uncle and cousin, many of the high-lights of the English theater were there, including Mrs. Patrick Campbell. They all knew I was broken-hearted about not being able to stay in London. They had been nice and kind, gentle and sympathetic, and even now, as I took my seat at the table, they were still nice and kind, gentle and sympathetic. I let them go on and didn't say a word, just keeping the contract where it was.

Finally Mrs. Campbell called down the table to me, "We are so sorry that you are sailing tomorrow."

Now was my time. "Oh, but I'm not," I said, as if it were the most casual announcement in the world.

Everybody at the table exclaimed and my uncle was the loudest of all. Uncle Jack said, "What-what-what-what?"

"I'm going to stay here," I said.

Uncle Jack asked, "What are you going to do?"

"Well, I have a very pleasant engagement," I replied. "I have just signed a contract with Sir Henry Irving and Miss Terry. I am going to be their leading lady."

Consternation! Not only for the family but for the whole table. And Mrs. Campbell.

III

The Newest Princess of Our Footlit Realm

I got the engagement with Irving in the late spring and it must have been some time toward the approach of mid-summer when I felt a sudden urge to go home and see Mummum before rehearsal for the new engagement began. But I had no money. I cabled to Dick Davis, asking him to send me $100. He was off to the wars somewhere, and it was his father who sent me the money, though I didn't know this until I began paying it back to Dick. And that was the first he ever knew about it. Mr. Davis hadn't bothered to tell him about that kindness to a little girl who had obviously needed it.

Mummum was at the Bevan House in Larchmont, quite alone except for Jack. I was very disturbed about her. She had no friends staying there. She used to sit on the porch hour after hour, day after day, looking out at nothing and I suppose remembering everything, occasionally reading little paper-back books that she brought down in quantities from her room on the third floor. I remember them so well, those paper-back novels with blue covers. I used to wonder if she was really reading them or just passing the time, turning over the pages while she was thinking of her great and crowded past.

She would come down in the morning and stay down until after dinner at night because it was too hard for her to climb those two flights of stairs—reading, rocking and thinking. I couldn't do anything about it then, with what was left of my borrowed $100, but I kept hoping that as soon as my wonderful ten pounds a week began coming in from Sir Henry, I could have her moved to a lower floor.

Mummum never talked about herself and it was hard to get her to talk about anything. I was sure, though, that she was pleased that I had come to see her. And her observations of the hotel and the people and of Larchmont in general were witty and penetrating. She missed nothing that went on, although apparently unaware of anything.

She seemed pleased that I was going to play with Irving, but she said rather cryptically, "Can you always understand what he says?"

I spent a week with her and then sailed back to my new and wonderful job. I went to stay a week or two with the Spenders (he was the editor of the *Westminster Gazette*) in Cheyne Walk, in Chelsea. The day I was to start rehearsals at the Lyceum the cable came, early in the morning. Mummum was dead.

There was much to be done, cables to be sent. Uncle Googan was in Australia. Uncle Jack was abroad. Lionel was on the road. At Larchmont there was only Jack, who at fourteen had to face what I had to face in California at the same age. Luckily my great-aunt Hannah, the sister of my grandfather John Drew, came forward and attended to everything.

But I was late for my first rehearsal. The old commissionaire at the stage door said with terrifying solemnity: "Oh, Missie, you're late!"

I flew onto the stage. There was all the company standing about and Sir Henry, sitting alone in the center of the stage looking at me under his eyebrows, very coldly.

I said, "Sir Henry, I'm dreadfully sorry to be late, but something terrible has happened."

Still looking at me under his eyebrows he said, "What was it?"

I said, "I just got a cable that my grandmother has died."

And his face, that beautiful face, looked up. He said, "Mrs. John Drew?" and I said, "Yes."

He said, "Go home, my dear. No rehearsal for you today."

That was the first of his many kindnesses to me.

I had a letter from my grandmother a week after she died, thanking me for having come to see her. It nearly broke my heart.

Soon afterward we went on a long tour in the provinces. Susanne Sheldon, another American girl, was in the company. Her mother was with her and together we lived in lodging houses on the road. Since I was getting the bigger salary, I paid for the sitting room which we all shared. Susanne had just gone on the stage and had a very small part, just walking on. I had never known her before, but she became a great friend of mine and we had funny experiences, going from place to place. All the members of the English company had booked lodgings far ahead and knew just where to go, but we foreigners in a strange land found ourselves two or three times in the most terrible places from which we had to go quickly. Some of the best-sounding addresses, "Something Crescents" or "Squares," turned out to be grim, but we were young and it was all exciting and wonderful.

Sir Henry was very serious and everybody else around the theater was frightened to death of him, but for some reason I always amused him. Something about me always made him laugh or smile. Later on, I often met him at big dinners where there were other important people, and how he stood out! How he made them all look commonplace, ordinary! He had the most delicate, beautiful face and beautiful, long hands.

I had no part in *The Merchant of Venice* so that I had many chances to see him in it. He always made Shylock seem the only gentleman in the play. I've always been glad, too, that I could so often see Ellen Terry as Portia.

During the tour we rehearsed *Peter the Great,* which was Laurence Irving's play. He had been tentatively marked for diplomatic service and had been sent to Russia as a sort of student guest of Tolstoy, who was a friend of his father. He was very Russian and very somber. I had never known any-one like that, so I was profoundly impressed and became Russian and somber, too. We had many melancholy walks through towns like Hull and Sheffield, which are suicidal anyway, and exactly suited our mood.

Then back to London, and Susanne and I took a flat together directly opposite the Websters' at 21 Bedford Street, Strand. The two lower floors were occupied by William Heinemann, the publisher, the two upper floors were ours. I had the room next to the drawing room and Susanne had a big one on the next floor, and we had a strange maid who had a strange little child who was kept strangely in the dark.

Laurence used to come to tea and gloom. He was a beau-tiful character; a little spasmodic and erratic but, underneath an assumed sinister manner, he was very gentle. I got his frame of mind and played nothing but Russian music of the most melancholy type. We floated together into a romance of Russian pessimism, of nervous depression. I decided that

I was as sad as Laurence, and to both of us life seemed very terrible. We thought we might just as well get married and be delightfully miserable together.

Laurence rushed off and announced our engagement to his father and mother, and there was a terrifying visit I had to make to Lady Irving. I don't remember ever meeting anyone as frightening. She and Sir Henry had been separated for years, and I felt so happy for him!

A curious thing about me at this time—and practically always—was that, in spite of the fact that I saw nothing of my father, or, shall I say, he saw nothing of me, I still had a strong urge to belong to someone, and there was now no one left but my father. So I cabled him at the Lambs Club, the only address I knew, telling him of my engagement. I received an answer saying:

CONGRATULATIONS LOVE FATHER

But the awful thing was that Laurence now became an entirely changed man. He was very happy and his happiness made him quite a different person, not the one whom I had agreed to marry and spend a long, lovely, gloomy, tragic life with. Of course it was all very young.

I was desolated but I knew I couldn't go on with the marriage and I had to tell Laurence that I'd made a terrible mistake. It required an enormous amount of courage to come to this decision, because there I was at the Lyceum Theatre in Laurence's play, with his father, and every hand would be against me. That I was prepared for—and how right I was! No one thought that I would have the courage to break the engagement. However I did.

Sir Henry was very kind and understanding about it, and later on, as the years went by, Laurence and I became the greatest friends. Also I was slightly comforted, after I had cabled my father that the engagement was broken, to receive a reply saying:

CONGRATULATIONS LOVE FATHER

But at the time I had to go on playing with the people who treated me like one of Laurence's lepers, and when Sir Henry gave a big supper party on the stage of the Lyceum after the first night of *Peter the Great,* I had to go to it. At the party a man I didn't know came up to me and said, "My dear child, you're the most natural thing I've ever seen on the stage."

Then he walked away and I asked someone who he was and he said: "That, my child, was Pinero."

That made a deep impression on me, but I didn't realize how deep until later on.

Dick Davis had come to London. One night he was driving me home from dinner at the McCarthys' and we got lost in a very thick fog. The cabman finally backed the hansom up on the sidewalk and its two wheels were wedged into the iron railings of a small house. We jumped out just as an oblong of light appeared, which turned out to be the front door, with two men and two women standing in it.

They invited us to come in and we did.

I don't know what put the idea into Dick's head but he began to address me as Duchess. I gasped but went along with it. The people were overawed; they went upstairs and brought the children down to see the young duchess, and after minute directions as to which turns to take we went out into the fog, followed by a chorus of "Good Night, Your Grace" in which the children's high voices joined.

We were lost again at once, but at last a boy with a torch leading the horse brought us back to the McCarthys', who put me up for the night. I was very thrilled by this ride because it seemed to take me back in the centuries. This experience gave Dick the idea for his famous story *In the Fog*.

A play came to London called *The Belle of New York*. On the night of the dress rehearsal I was not in our play at the Lyceum so I went to the rehearsal because Phyllis Rankin, Aunt Gladys's sister, was in it. I was sitting alone in the dark theater when I heard three managers, two Australians and an Englishman, telling Mr. Lederer, the producer:

"You can't open this play in London tomorrow night. The British audience wouldn't understand a word of it. It's too American."

Mr. Lederer walked out into the dark lobby and paced up and down looking very worried and I, being terribly young, had courage enough to go up to him and say: "Please don't believe them. I'm sure they'll love it just as it is. They'll love it so much that if they don't understand it, they'll come again and again and again till they do, and in the meantime they'll be loving it!"

He said, "Who on earth are you?"

And I said, "Oh, I'm not anybody, but I just *know*. Please, please don't change it!"

I must have been very fierce and eager, as usual. At any rate he didn't change a word. It opened the next night and ran for years and years and everybody in London was quoting from it, sometimes quite wrong, but nevertheless learning a new language and loving it.

I gave a tea party, a big one, in our flat for *The Belle of New York* people. Edna May was there and Phyllis Rankin and a lot of others. Jack, who had been sent to a school in England by my father, was at the flat, but he was too shy to come downstairs to the party. I said, "You've got to," but he wouldn't. He broke out into a cold sweat, and I didn't ask him any more.

This terror of people and gatherings left him at an early age.

He went back to school but he managed to get away from it when he pleased—he had invented a major, supposed to be a friend of father's, who demanded Jack's presence quite often. Later he studied at the Slade School of Art, living at Aunt Eva Wace's.

Mr. John Hay was now Ambassador to the Court of St. James's, and every Thursday afternoon I would go to the Embassy to help Helen and Alice pour tea and make myself useful in any way I could. I remember Helen saying to me, "Don't you find when you go out to dinner in London that you have to take with you everything you ever knew or ever read to be able to cope with the brilliant young men?"

And you did. You had to cope with really brilliant young men just out of Oxford or Cambridge and probably already in Parliament.

It was the fashion then to wear tiaras and of course I

didn't have one. So instead I got some oak leaves and wore them in my hair. Somebody called me Daphne, and soon everybody was calling me that. I had always hated Ethel as a name—my father had called me that after Thackeray's Ethel Newcome—and I loved being called Daphne. One of those who always called me Daphne was Gerald du Maurier, who named his younger daughter Daphne after me.

I went out to lots of dinners and dances—sometimes two or three a night during the season. One evening I went to dinner at the Heinemanns'. There were only eight people there but one of them was Whistler. He had one of his great evenings and no one else spoke. It was absolutely breathtaking for me. When I got home I had to wake Susanne up to tell her all about it.

Susanne fell very much in love with a man who believed in free love, which in those days was talked about very freely, and she decided that she would go and live with him, but being a Vermonter with a Vermonter's conscience, she felt that she must go home and tell her mother about it. When she came back within a month, she found that her man was living in that wonderful free love—with another woman.

Some years later she married a very beautiful young man named Henry Ainley, who played Paolo in Stephen Phillips' *Paolo and Francesca*. The wedding took place under a great tree in a meadow, at the home of Mr. and Mrs. William Faversham, at Chiddingfold. At the wedding Anthony Hope, who was a friend of both Susanne's and Henry's, suddenly saw, crossing the lawn to him, his

Princess Flavia, straight from Zenda. She was Susanne's
lovely young sister, just arrived from America. She had
masses of red hair; it wasn't long before they were married.

Life in London was very gay and very stimulating and
very glamorous and yet, young though I was, I took it as a
matter of course. It is curious but the only place where I was
never terribly shy was in England. Once in New York when
Mr. Whitney was giving a ball for Dorothy, his youngest
daughter, I got a lovely new dress at Bendel's to wear. That
night I drove up to the great Whitney house, but instead
of going in, I said to my driver, "Go home." In London I
could go to Buckingham Palace and think nothing of it.

It has never mattered to me who anybody was. Mr. Frohman once said to me, "You're the funniest girl! One day
you walk in here with Sam Bernard and the next day with a
duchess!"

"Why not?" I said. "I know them both."

I didn't feel any different about going to a great ball at
which royalty was present than about playing in Wilkes-
Barre. Margot Asquith of the acid tongue once said, "No
one has ever done anything like what Ethel's done in
London."

But I was never aware that I was breaking records. I just
took it for granted that everybody had as good a time as I was
having. Doors opened without my knowing that they were
ever closed and I just walked through them.

No wonder I never wanted to leave it!

But at the Websters' I had met Gerald du Maurier, who
was so entirely different from Laurence Irving that I found
him enchanting. He was tall and slight, not good looking,

but with great charm, gay, amusing, witty. He *swept* me and I thought, *"This is it!"* So Gerald and I were engaged. (I didn't have to cable father this time for he was in London and I went to see him for a minute.)

Gerald's mother was divine to me and so were his sisters. One of them, Sylvia, was very beautiful. Her father, George du Maurier, had often drawn her to illustrate his books; she looked exactly like the picture of the Duchess of Towers in *Peter Ibbetson*. (Sylvia was married to Llewelyn Davies and they had four or five sons. It was for these children that Barrie really invented *Peter Pan*—the eldest one was named Peter.) Another sister was Trixie, who was beautiful in a different way from Sylvia and another one was May; and they were an utterly enchanting family. But in spite of all their kindness to me, when Mrs. du Maurier began to tell me how to take care of Gerald, what to make him wear in winter and so on, it all alarmed me so that all I could think of was getting home to the four walls of my dressing room— any dressing room. I had just enough money for cheap passage back to America by Canada and for the night train to New York. Gerald saw me off at the train. I felt heart-broken. I was crying, tears pouring down my cheeks. Gerald was running along the platform. I almost jumped off the train. I was still in love with Gerald, but I knew I couldn't go through with the marriage.

It was not a very happy trip for me. I was leaving the city I loved; everything I cared about seemed to be concentrated there. I was going to something that didn't even exist, for, after all, that's what a position that you haven't really got is.

And so I arrived at Grand Central Terminal with exactly

one quarter in my bag, all that I had left. This I grandly gave the red cap who carried my bag to the hansom.

I had no idea where I was going or what was to happen to me, and out of a maze of bewilderment a voice from the top of the cab came through with, "Where to, miss?" For some reason I said, "The Waldorf," which at that time was perhaps the most expensive hotel in the world.

Penniless and with head very high, I went up to the desk of the Waldorf, rather frightened and wondering what was going to happen to me next, but putting on a bold front. I was absolutely staggered by four or five young clerks coming forward and greeting me with enthusiasm and a certain amount of ceremony. For a moment I thought they must have mistaken me for someone else until they said: "Miss Barrymore, we are so glad to have you back with us again."

I said, "Oh," faintly, and then added, "I just want to know if my uncle is here."

"Oh, yes, Mr. Drew is here. Will you want a suite or—?"

"I'll have a room," I said.

The porter brought me back to life again: "The cab is waiting."

I said, "Oh, yes," rather languidly and then turned to one of the clerks: "Will you pay my cab, please?"

I followed the bellboy to my room and as the door closed and I was left alone I felt something that I had not expected to feel. I sat down on a chair with the realization that I had come home, that this was my country, my land, and the words of welcome that I got from the porters, cabmen and clerks was something that made the life I had just left in London quite unreal. I felt that welcome and warmth which can come only from your own people. Here was where I belonged. I had come home.

Later I found out the reason for the overwhelming reception. The American newspapers, which I had not seen in London, had been full of me and of the parties I had been going to. Besides the two real engagements, they had made up others—dukes and earls and even an Indian prince whom I had never seen. Of course at the time I knew nothing about all this. All I knew was that I was being greeted as if I were a great personage when I wasn't anybody. But I remember that it was comforting at the moment.

Immediately I called Uncle Jack's room.

"Who on earth is this?" he asked. "It sounds like Ethel."

"It is!" I said.

"But you're in England!" he insisted.

"No," I said, "I'm upstairs in the hotel."

After I had convinced him that I really was upstairs and not in London he told me to come down and have breakfast with him.

So I did and while we were having the best breakfast I had had for many a long day I told him that I had come home to try to get an engagement. I asked if he would take me to see Mr. Frohman.

He said, "Well, well, we'll have to see."

Although I had been under Mr. Frohman's management all the while I was with my uncle, I did not know him at all

and was very much in awe of him. I would not have dared
go to see him alone.

We went the next day. It was the first time I had ever
been in the office where I was destined to spend so many,
many hours in the years to come. Mr. Frohman was very
nice to me, said I looked like my mother, who had played
with him and of whom he was always very fond, and he
added: "There is a part in Annie Russell's new play,
Catherine. It isn't much of a part—"

I replied that I would be satisfied with anything, that I
was very much broke and that anything would mean a great
deal to me. So I was told to be at rehearsal the next day at
the Garrick Theatre.

When I arrived there I found it was indeed a very small
part, calling for two beautiful dresses but not much else!
I had to pay for them out of my salary of $35 a week. They
cost $100 apiece and it took me all season to pay for them.
One of the sad things about the theater is that when you are
beginning, trying to make a very little money go a long
way, you have to pay for your own clothes; when you're a
star, relatively rich, they're provided for you.

I summoned courage to ask for an advance on my salary
so I could get out of the Waldorf and move back to Mrs.
Wilson's boardinghouse where I had lived before.

When I walked onto the stage the first night of that
play, *Catherine*, I got the most tremendous ovation, and I
kept saying to myself, "This is awful. I have nothing to do
—just two or three lines in this act and two or three in the
next!"

It was dreadful, getting that enormous amount of ap-

Miss Barrymore as Mme. Trentoni, her first starring role, in *Captain Jinks of the Horse Marines* (Culver Service)

A scene from *Captain Jinks of the Horse Marines* with (left to right) Sydney Cowell, Fanny Addison Pitt, Miss Barrymore and H. Reeves-Smith (Culver Service)

A Scrap of Paper with (left to right) Mary Boland, Charles Dalton, Ethel Barrymore and John Drew (Culver Service)

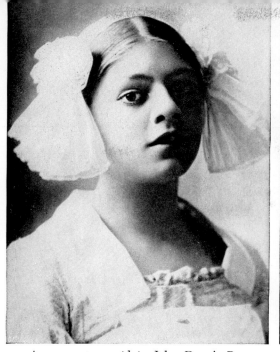

As a country maid in John Drew's *Rose-mary*, 1896 (Culver Service)

With Gerald Du Maurier in *Cynthia* (Culver Service)

In the costume she wore in *Alice-Sit-by-the-Fire* (Culver Service)

Cousin Kate (Culver Service)

With Sir Winston Churchill at
Blenheim Palace

Miss Barrymore in *Catherine*

Ethel Barrymore in *Carrots* (Culver Service)

In her dressing room during *Carrots* (Culver Service)

As Lady Helen Haden in *Déclassée*

A scene from *Trelawny of the Wells*
with Constance Collier
(Culver Service)

Miss Barrymore with Eric Maturin in *Mid-Channel,* 1910 (Courtesy, Museum of the City of New York)

John and Ethel Barrymore in *A Slice of Life* (Spencer Berger Collection)

A scene from *Our Mrs. McChesney*,
1915 (Culver Service)

In *Our Mrs. McChesney*
(Culver Service)

plause, standing there and knowing that nothing in the part would live up to it. I still had no idea that anyone over here knew about my life in England or bothered about me. I will never forget the agony of that big ovation with nothing in my part to warrant it, except those two pretty dresses.

One newspaper critic made the momentous discovery that I was "rather disappointing." But some yellow journal called me "that glamour girl." It was the first time I had ever seen or heard the word. Years afterward Neysa McMein and I were talking about the debutantes who were being given terrific balls that cost thousands of dollars, and I said, "What do they mean by glamour girl?"

Neysa said, "You should ask!"

And then I remembered back to those London days.

In *Catherine* Annie Russell played a part in which the master of a great house engaged her as governess to his daughters. At the end of the first act he asked her to play Chopin's Nocturne on the piano, which she was supposed to teach his daughters to play. But Annie Russell could not play the piano, so she sat at a dummy one and I played for her, offstage. I had very little to do in the play, so I used to sit in my dressing room and read until a boy would come and say "music." Then I would dash up, play and go back to my book.

One night the boy didn't come. That was no excuse for me, of course. I should have been listening, but I had depended upon him for weeks. I didn't know what had happened until the curtain was down. I'll never forget the look Annie Russell gave me as our eyes met.

I could only gasp, "Oh, I am so sorry! It is terrible!" All she said was, "Yes, it is," and went to her room.

I felt as if an elevator had dropped from under me. I haven't got over it yet—I still wake up in the night and think of it.

They didn't do anything to me, but they got someone else to play the piano.

Cecil Clark was about to marry Dick Davis, and while *Catherine* was playing in Chicago, we had our dresses for the wedding made at the same place. The marriage took place at Marion early in May. Dick had his brother Charles as his best man, and a lot of his friends for ushers, but I was the only bridesmaid.

Dick gave me a very handsome diamond brooch in the form of a buckle as my bridesmaid's present, and I was thrilled by it. And more than once, later on, when I came home penniless from a London summer, that brooch kept me alive until I was working again. I never will forget how frightened and guilty I felt the first time I pawned it at Simpson's just around the corner from the boardinghouse, but I got bravely over that as soon as I realized they didn't think I was a second-story man. The visit to the pawnshop came to be an autumnal habit. Of course as soon as I was working, the first thing I would do would be to redeem the brooch.

When *Catherine* ended its run, I had saved enough to go back to England in June, besides paying for those two dresses, which, because I had paid for them myself, I could take with me.

I went to England on *The Paris* of the American Line,

which was largely owned by Mr. Griscom of Philadelphia, whose son Lloyd was a great friend of Dick Davis's and one of the three gringos in Dick's book, *Three Gringos in Venezuela.* Mr. and Mrs. Griscom were on board *The Paris* with their daughter Pansy, who was a friend of mine, and they insisted that I sit at their table. Although they were Quakers and "theed" each other all the time, Mr. Griscom had a terrible temper, and at almost every meal there would be an explosion that would end in his firing a steward, for some such crime as serving soup that Mr. Griscom didn't think was hot enough. Then he would turn solemnly to his wife and say, "Is thee all right, dearie?"

I got lodgings at 18-A Clifford Street and began at once to have good times with old friends and to make new ones. One of these was the Earl of Ava, who called me Cinderella. He was terribly nice, and so were his two brothers, Terence and Basil Blackwood. Basil did all of the illustrations for Hilaire Belloc's *A Bad Child's Book of Beasts.* I'll never forget the illustration for the verse about the yak, and I can still recite the poem itself.

> As a friend to the children commend me the Yak.
> You'll find it exactly the thing:
> It will carry and fetch,
> You can ride on its back,
> Or lead it about with a string.
> The Tartar who dwells on the plains of Thibet,
> (A desolate region of snow)
> Has for centuries made it a nursery pet,
> And surely the Tartar should know!

I wrote a note to Basil in verse.

> Oh, most foolish BTB
> Come and take a walk with me
> In the park this afternoon
> Not too late and not too soon
> As I must hie to many teas
> I rather think that three-thirtee's
> The time for you to come and say
> At the door of 18-A
> Is the foolish maiden in?
> And the menial with a grin
> Unless with all her main and might
> She's been and died within the night.

When he called for me, I asked him how he liked my poem, and he said, "What poem?"

For a while that summer Jack and I had rooms in a cottage at Cookham across the river from Taplow. One day Jack said he had invited Tod Sloan to come to tea and asked me if I minded. I thought he was joking, but Sloan came. He turned out to be a little man with the most gigantic conceit I ever came across—so colossal that he wasn't even amusing. Jack was sorry he had brought him.

At first everybody in England laughed at Sloan's way of riding perched out on the horse's neck, but he won so many races that they not only changed their minds but their methods.

Among the new friends I made that summer was Millie, the Duchess of Sutherland. I was often at Stafford House, the great town house on which the Sutherlands had a ninety-nine-year lease. Besides Millie's three children, Geordie, Alistair and Rosemary, the children of the Duke's sister also grew up in Stafford House. After their mother died, their father, Mr. Chaplin, came to live there and brought Florence, Edie and Eric with him. Lady Constance Mac-Kenzie, another niece of the Duke, also grew up in Stafford House.

In August I went to Dunrobin, the Sutherlands' fabulous place at the very top of Scotland. There were thousands and thousands of acres surrounding a great castle with terrace after terrace of lawn and flowers going down to the sea. It was just before a big party, and there were only a few of us there, Millie, her children, Florence Chaplin, Constance MacKenzie and me. After dinner the children said, "Let's play charahdes."

I said, "NO!"

Millie said, "Very well, we won't play charahdes, but I have something wonderful to read. Ethel will love it because it's American."

And she proceeded to read, getting the accents all wrong, a George Ade fable. The children laughed at all the wrong places, but they loved it.

It was the first of many wonderful times at Dunrobin. Margot and Henry Asquith (his name was Herbert Henry and in public life he was known as H. H., but all his friends called him Henry), who had rented a place near Aberdeen, had asked me to stay with them on my way back to London, and I traveled down with Evan Charteris, arriving at Aberdeen in a pouring rain to find that there was nothing to meet us. Evan was furious, but I thought it was funny and so like Margot. We finally hired a cab, which took us to a horror of a chocolate castle, apparently empty. Evan began shouting and finally Margot appeared with a bridge score in her hand. She said, "Oh, I thought it was tomorrow."

Henry had not yet come in from golf.

Such wonderful dinners at Margot's with those interesting and exciting people! I nearly always sat next to Henry Asquith at these parties. He used to say, "Put Ethel next to me. It's all right to put one of those duchesses on my right, but I want Ethel on my left."

On the other side of me would be Chesterton or Balfour —once, I remember, Lord Rosebery. I can't think of them all now, but as Helen Hay once said, when you go out to dinner in England, you must take with you all you have in the way of mentality, for you are sure to need it.

Once Henry Asquith turned to me at dinner and said, "Tell me, Ethel, have you ever heard of an American named Alexander Hamilton?"

I said, "Henry, you're not really asking me that, are you?"

"Yes," he said.

I said, "Have you ever heard of an American named George Washington?"

He had just been reading Gertrude Atherton's book, *The Conqueror*, which is about Alexander Hamilton.

Margot came from a politically conservative family. When she married Henry, who was a Liberal, there were some of her old dowager relatives who regarded him as fifty years later they would have regarded a member of the Labour Party. They expected him to be almost a hod carrier instead of a brilliant Balliol man that he was.

While we were at the chocolate castle, Evan Charteris took us over to see his father, Lord Wemyss, who had a place nearby—a delightful old gentleman of ninety. He had a "Mona Lisa" which he insisted was the real one. The one in the Louvre, he said, was a copy. We were all polite and agreed with him.

I also stayed with Alfred and Didi Littleton who had taken a small house in Scotland. Arthur Balfour was the only other person staying with them. They were all crazy about bridge, and I had to play with them although I didn't know how. It was agonizing but they were very kind.

Later I stayed with Herbert and Dolly Gladstone, who had rented a furnished house with a harmonium in it. I used to play it after dinner, and we would sing hymns.

By the end of summer my savings were gone once more and Mr. Lestocq, who was Mr. Frohman's London manager, provided me with transportation home as he was to do after so many later summers.

In New York I went back to Mrs. Wilson's and my diamond buckle made its first acquaintance with Simpson's pawnshop. Charles Frohman was putting on *His Excellency the Governor* which I had seen in London and I was fired with ambition to play Irene Vanbrugh's part in it.

Although frightened to death, I managed to muster up enough courage to see Mr. Frohman and ask him about it. I was really shaking all over. I remember having to hold my hands together so that Mr. Frohman would not see how I was trembling, as I said, "I hear you are going to do *His Excellency the Governor*. I want to play Stella."

Mr. Frohman replied: "Do you, indeed? So does Ellen Terry."

"Oh!" I gasped.

He seemed very much amused and said, "Well, I don't think you can play a part like that quite yet, but if you like you can study it and rehearse it for me someday."

So they gave me the part and I studied it. One morning I told him that I was ready for the rehearsal he had promised me. Although I think he had forgotten all about his promise, he very kindly and patiently went downstairs in the Empire Theatre and sat in the dark, empty auditorium while I went on a fairly dark stage. As there was only one little light, the stage manager, who was holding the book and giving me the lines, could scarcely see. I had to attempt a performance of a brilliant, sparkling comedy part almost in the dark, to an audience of one! An awful occasion! After it was all over, Mr. Frohman was very nice and again told me that I reminded him very much of my mother—in fact, that I was amazingly like her. This naturally made me happy.

About two days after my rehearsal before Mr. Frohman I read the announcement of the play's forthcoming production at the Empire and I need hardly say that I was not in the cast. But later on in the season, when the play was through its New York run and Mr. Frohman was about to send it on the road, he told me that he would let me play the part if I really thought I could. Of course I said that I was sure I could, and so we started off on tour.

The part I was playing was that of a comedy adventuress. I was, of course, much too young for it, so I got myself a beautiful red wig and a black-spangled dress and thought myself quite the real thing. It was a strenuous tour, with a stretch of one-night stands eight weeks in succession. But I thrived on it, since I was playing a role I loved and everything was very nice. I was getting eighty dollars a week. Mr. Frohman was much pleased with my notices; everywhere I went the critics were as kind as they could be. The week we were playing in Brooklyn Mr. Frohman let me have a special matinee in New York, an invitation performance. I really cannot remember very much about it—not even what the object was or what came out of it. But as my memory of it is fairly comfortable, I suppose it was all right.

It was while I was playing in *His Excellency* that I suddenly discovered that instead of making a comedy point, I was throwing it away—tossing it off—as if it meant nothing, thus achieving much more successfully the effect that I wanted. I had seen my mother do this when she came to Philadelphia in *The Senator* with William H. Crane, when I had realized her wonderful naturalness and ease.

Nobody in our family ever taught me anything about acting except by absorption, but in our family absorption was a good way to learn. I remembered my grandmother; I remembered, without having realized it till now, the naturalness of my mother's acting, twenty-five years ahead of her time. I had played for three years with Uncle Jack, who acted so naturally that he never seemed to be acting, so naturally that he never let anyone see a wheel going around.

In *His Excellency* I began to understand the necessity of covering up those wheels, of never letting one of them show, no matter what the critics might say, no matter if some wheely actresses seemed to be successful. And I began to think, too, that this was what Pinero had meant.

I loved *His Excellency* and I played it everywhere for a whole season.

On a train from Wilkes-Barre to Scranton, the man in front of me was reading a newspaper and I saw big headlines saying AMERICAN GIRL WILL BECOME MARCHIONESS OF DUF-FERIN AND AVA, which meant that Lord Ava was dead and that Terence, his younger brother, who was married to Flora Davis, would inherit the title when his father died. Lord Ava had gone to the Boer War and had been killed at Lady-smith.

During the run of *His Excellency the Governor*, I man-aged to save enough money for a holiday and so, at the end of the season, I went back to England to spend my summer vacation.

When I got to London I went right from the boat train to see Mr. Frohman at the Savoy Hotel and he said, "Where are you going to live?"

I said, "I don't know yet."

"You had better get a room here," he said.

I said, "I can't afford that."

"Never mind," he said, "get a room here. You can't be roaming around."

But the next day Millie Sutherland said, "You can't live at the Savoy Hotel all by yourself. Come and stay at Stafford House."

So I went to live in that vast Victorian pile. It was like living in Buckingham Palace. There was room in it for half a dozen families. Besides Millie and the Duke and their three children, Mr. Chaplin and his three children were living there.

Mr. Chaplin was quite old and formal and yet so gay. It was wonderful to hear him talk. He would send his servant up to me with a note, asking if I was going to be in that evening and would do him the honor of dining with him. I would send back word that I would be delighted, and we would dine in the great dining room at a small table with several footmen waiting on us. Then he would say good night and go upstairs in his elevator.

London was not so gay as it had been the year before; many of the people I knew had lost husbands or sons or brothers in the Boer War, which was still going badly. Nevertheless, I had a wonderful time seeing my old friends and making new ones and going to the theater—and how I loved going to the theater in London.

I kept on meeting interesting people like Hilaire Belloc and Chesterton and Mr. Lucey, a charming man who wrote for *Punch*. The Farjeons, who were nieces and nephews of Joseph Jefferson, took me to Alma-Tadema's and to Burne-Jones's and other places where otherwise I might never have gone. Once when I'd met Richard Strauss I felt as if I'd been in the presence of a divinity. And it was exciting to meet Max Beerbohm, whose writing I tremendously admired, but one person who filled me with complete horror was George Moore. He was like something under a stone.

I remember that one night Millie took me to dine with Alfred Rothschild. He had a perfectly wonderful octagonal dining room with a painting of a beautiful woman set into each of the eight paneled walls. Years and years later when

I went to see the Huntington collection in Pasadena, some of the pictures suddenly made me see again a pale yellow octagonal room. I said to Mr. Hapgood, "Of course Duveen, but where else did those pictures come from?"

And he said, "Duveen bought them from the people to whom Alfred Rothschild had disposed of them thirty-five years ago."

Jack was eighteen that summer and he came with me when I went to stay with Millie at Dunrobin, that wonderful place of the Sutherlands on the sea. It was a very big houseparty. The Grenfells were there with their five children. Winston Churchill and Harry Percy were there, too. I was always fascinated by Harry's name. It sounded so Shakespearean.

I remember Jack's delight the first night at dinner when the Earl of Mar and Kellie appeared in a gorgeous kilt. Just after we had been seated—there must have been forty of us at table—a most piercing shriek came from behind the duke's chair. Nobody paid any attention to it but went on talking—all except Jack and me. We glanced at each other with expressions of horror. Then we saw something move back of the duke's chair. It was the piper. He began to stalk majestically around the table, piping the most pitiful sounds. As no one paid any attention to him, Jack and I realized that it must be a well-known custom, not to be noticed.

We had splendid swimming up there. As a great many of the tenants were fishermen, and as it is a surprising fact that very few fishermen can swim, Millie was anxious that they should all learn and had imported a magnificent Swede to act as their instructor. The Swede made a large diving float for us and we used to have wonderful exhibitions of diving by the Swede, Constance MacKenzie and Florence Chaplin. Constance was the most beautiful swimmer I have ever seen. Jack, incidentally, was very good. He had never dived from any great height before, but he could not bear to see two girls doing it, so off he went one day and made the best dive of anybody—a way Jack had.

He had a wonderful time at Dunrobin, and at the end of the summer he came back to America with me. I was determined that in the future America would be my place for work, but that every summer I would go back to England and enjoy myself.

Of course I went directly to Mr. Frohman as soon as I returned from England; it never entered my head to go to see any other manager as long as he lived. At that time Clyde Fitch was becoming more and more popular and successful as a dramatist. He had already several successful plays running in New York. Mr. Frohman told me about a new play of Mr. Fitch's he was going to produce, *Captain Jinks of the Horse Marines*, which had a wonderful part in it. But he was not at all sure that I could play it; nor was Mr. Fitch— particularly Mr. Fitch. However, Mr. Frohman decided to take a chance with me, and we began rehearsals. The role was that of Madame Trentoni, very taxing for so young and inexperienced an actress. There were comedy, pathos and dancing in it. I was more worried about the dancing than about anything else.

We opened in Philadelphia, in the Walnut Street Theatre. I was terrified, and a voice from the gallery called out, "Speak up, Ethel, you Drews is all good actors."

When I got back to the Stenton Hotel where I was living, some of my friends assured me that everything had gone splendidly. I said, "Yes, I feel so, too." But I wondered what the newspapers would say the next morning.

The notices were amazingly bad—fairly bad for the play and very bad for me. One woman critic wrote: "If the young lady who plays Madame Trentoni had possessed beauty, charm or talent, this play might have been a success"—the only criticism I have ever been able to remember word for word.

I was crushed. All through the run in Philadelphia and the two weeks of one-night stands that followed I was feeling numb, hoping and praying that we would close permanently. I begged Mr. Frohman not to take the play to New York. But we went on one-night stands for another week and during that week we heard that we were to come into New York for a fortnight only. Mr. Fitch wanted it. He already had two plays running successfully in New York, so I suppose he thought he could afford to chance a failure.

We opened at the Garrick Theatre on February 4, 1901. The advertisements announced: "For two weeks only. A play by Clyde Fitch called *Captain Jinks of the Horse Marines.*"

On the opening night I had for the first time the terrible sense of responsibility which, ever since, has made every first night a kind of little dying, an agony of terror that never failed to make me physically sick. While I had been playing small parts, and even in *His Excellency*, I hadn't been important enough to have that terrific feeling of responsibility. Even in *Captain Jinks* in Philadelphia and on

GARRICK THEATRE

HOYT & McKEE,
Lessees,
Also Lessees Madison Square Theatre.

CHARLES FROHMAN, Manager,
Also Manager of the Empire, Criterion, Garden and Madison
Square Theatres, New York City, and the
DUKE OF YORK'S and VAUDEVILLE THEATRES, LONDON, ENG.

Evenings, 8.30.   Matinees Wednesday and Saturday, at 2.15.

CHARLES FROHMAN presents

A Fantastic Comedy in Three Acts, entitled

Captain Jinks of the Horse Marines

By CLYDE FITCH.
WITH
ETHEL BARRYMORE.

THE PERSONS CONCERNED IN THE PLAY:

CAPTAIN ROBERT CARROLTON JINKS	GEORGE W. HOWARD
CHARLES LAMARTINE	FRANCIS BYRNE
AUGUSTUS BLEEKER VON VORKENBERG	H. S. TABOR
PROFESSOR BELLIARTI	GEORGE W. BARNUM
THE HERALD REPORTER	JOHN R. SUMNER
THE TRIBUNE REPORTER	CHARLES MARRIOTT
THE TIMES REPORTER	HARRY E. ASMUS
THE SUN REPORTER	WM. BARSTOW SMITH
THE CLIPPER REPRESENTATIVE	GARDNER JENKINS
A NEWSBOY	HARRY BARTON
AN OFFICIAL DETECTIVE	LEWIS WOOD
A SAILOR	LORENZO HALE
A POLICEMAN	M. J. GALLAGHER
A TELEGRAPH BOY	JOHN HUGHES
MRS. GREENBOROUGH	ESTELLE MORTIMER
MRS. JINKS	MRS. ANNIE ADAMS
MRS. STONINGTON	FANNY ADDISON PITT
MISS MERRIAM	SYDNEY COWELL
FIRST BALLET LADY (Miss Pettitoes)	LILLIAN THURGATE
SECOND BALLET LADY	MARGARET DUNNE
THIRD BALLET LADY	EVELYN JEPSON
FOURTH BALLET LADY (Frauline Hochspitz)	ANITA ROTHE
FIFTH BALLET LADY	ANNA MORRISON
SIXTH BALLET LADY (Mrs. Maggitt)	KATE TEN EYCK
SEVENTH BALLET LADY	ALICE BRYAN
MARY	BEATRICE AGNEW

AND

MME. TRENTONI (Aurelia Johnson)	ETHEL BARRYMORE

Domestics, Sailors, etc.

New York City in the early Seventies.

Programme continued on second page following.

tour afterward, I had barely begun to feel it. It was only on
the opening night in New York that I really felt the full
weight of it and began to suffer as I have every first night.
I think I have always managed to hide it from the audience
but I don't know how I've lived through it.

I kept saying to myself, as I have done on every first night
since, "Why am I doing this? Why didn't I try to do something else?" I would have been glad of an earthquake or
some other great calamity that would stop people from coming in or me from going on.

But the terror I felt that night in *Captain Jinks* was only
a beginning, a minor thing compared to what it grew into.
Years and years afterward on the first night of *The Corn Is
Green*, although I knew it was a wonderful, beautiful play
and that I was all right in it, I was still hoping for an
earthquake.

Once someone said to my son Jackie, "Do you think
you've inherited any of your mother's talent?"

"I don't know," he said, "but I think I've inherited some
of her terror."

But the opening night of *Captain Jinks,* in spite of my
sick anguish of panic, was one of those unexpected, sensa-
tional successes.

My father came backstage after the play. There were
crowds of people on the stage, so he just kissed me and said,
"It was wonderful, darling," and faded away.

The next day the critics were even more enthusiastic than
the audience had been. One of them wrote:

Last night Mr. Charles Frohman was our host at a proud occasion. Last night hosannas rang through the town. Not since John

Drew led Ada Rehan before the curtain at Mr. Daly's has there been such cause for hurraying, such kidglove-bursting applause, such bouquet tossing across the bedazzled footlights, welcoming our youngest, our newest, our dearest star, Miss Ethel Barrymore, as "Madame Trentoni" in Mr. Clyde Fitch's fanciest fancy, "Captain Jinks of the Horse Marines." . . . Today Herald Square will be a wild hurly-burly of ticket buyers lining up at the beaming, bustling box office at the Garrick. . . . Lucky people. Lucky public to have Miss Ethel Barrymore—to be trampled to death—for New York is at your feet! Dear Ethel. Dear Miss Barrymore. Dear Miss Ethel Barrymore—newest princess of our footlit realm.

Thank God Clyde Fitch had vanity!

I was still living at Mrs. Wilson's boardinghouse and Jack had come to live there, too. I now moved from the hall bedroom to the second-floor front. A very grand move, indeed, as I had an alcove to my bedroom and this made me think I had a sitting room. I was getting $125 a week and thought myself very fortunate. The fact that several other members of the company were getting much bigger salaries did not worry me.

Mrs. Wilson's house was on Thirty-sixth Street and the Garrick on Thirty-fifth Street. I used to walk around to the theater every night along Sixth Avenue. One evening Jack walked around the corner with me. As we approached the theater—I had been playing about a month—the lights in the front of the house looked different to me. I did not pay much attention to them as I was thinking about something else. But I sensed that there was a change somewhere and I glanced up again and suddenly stood frozen to the spot.

ETHEL BARRYMORE was up there in lights.

Next day I went to see Mr. Frohman to thank him. He

waved his hand toward the people passing by in the street. "I didn't do it," he said. "They did it."

The play ran for months. Every night the old-fashioned bouquet of gardenias that I carried when I went on stage in my white dress in the last act came to me at the theater with a card on which was written "L'inconnu." It was years before I found out who it was who sent them.

Later, when we were on tour, there was a man who always bought two tickets in the front row, one for his hat and coat and one for himself. This started in Cleveland, but he would suddenly appear in other cities. He wrote mad letters and kept sending me diamond pins and bracelets, and in sending them back I learned about registered mail.

It's curious how you dare to go on the stage knowing there's an eccentric in the audience who might shoot you. You have to think of it but not too much or you wouldn't be able to go on.

New York was very kind to me all that winter. I was young and healthy, so I was able to combine work and play pretty well. Although I enjoyed going out very much, I still was just as happy at Mrs. Wilson's, having crackers and milk after the theater and talking to my cousin, Georgie Drew Mendum.

While we were playing in New York I would have Frances Rosengarten and Dora Harris to lunch in the Palm Room of the old Waldorf. Oscar always saved one corner table for me. We used to call the Waldorf "The Habit" because we went there so often. Frances and Dora and the Tysons in Philadelphia and I had a sort of language that nobody else could understand. It sounded like English, but it was a completely foreign language to anybody except us. Frances had a lot of expressions, too, that were just her own. Once she sent me a telegram saying, "Will be crouching in the front row. Chin resting."

When Dora Harris married Douglas Cox and went to live in Llewellyn Park, I used to go over there and see her. Thomas Edison lived next door and I often saw him puttering about, very sweet, very deaf, very kind. It gave me a thrill just to be on the same level ground with him.

After a while Arthur Brisbane gave Jack a job, drawing a picture a week for the New York *Journal*. Brisbane thought so highly of the drawings that he paid Jack $50 a week, and Jack left the boardinghouse and took rooms with a red-haired reporter from St. Louis who was getting $35 a week on the *World*. His name was Herbert Bayard Swope.

About this time Kathleen Neilson's mother, who lived in a big house at 100 Fifth Avenue, decided that I must come and stay there for a while. I had to share Kathleen's room, but that was fine. She was a sweet girl. She was engaged to a boy at Yale, and every single night she would sit up and write to him. Then she would wake up her Nounou, her French nurse, who would have to put on her clothes and go out and post the letter. I can remember wondering what on earth Kathleen could think of to fill up all those pages every night. The boy was Reggie Vanderbilt, whom she married as soon as he was graduated.

Mrs. Neilson was a character, different from anybody I ever knew. She was the first woman I ever heard swear— really swear—quite casually. She used to take me for drives in her beautiful, perfectly appointed victoria and she'd say to the driver when he stopped at a crossing, "God damn it! Why do we have to stop here?"

I remember that once when she and I were in the front drawing room and Reggie and Kathleen were in the back drawing room sitting on the piano bench talking, Mrs. Neilson said, "What the hell do you suppose those two fools find to talk about?"

In the spring we went on tour. What I remember about that tour is sitting on the back platform of the train and seeing little lambs and colts and dogwoods and blossoms— just spring. I don't think spring can be more beautiful anywhere in the world than in upper New York and Pennsylvania.

Willie Frank, who had started as Mr. Frohman's office boy, got his first chance to be a company manager with me in *Captain Jinks*. He was with me for twenty years, and in fact was with me when he died in his berth on a train.

The stage manager was James Kearney, and his wife had a part in the play. They were with me for twenty years, he as my stage manager and she in the play whenever I could find a part for her. It was a wonderful thing for me to have them with me. They became almost like a part of my family. After Mr. Kearney, Eddie McHugh was my stage manager for another twenty years. Bruce McRae was my leading man for seven. I always tried to keep the same people around me if I could, and we were always a happy lot of people.

The play ran on into the summer—I remember that we played a Fourth of July matinee—and we didn't close long enough for me to go to England. Instead I went to stay at Marion with the Davises and at Beverly Farms with Mr. and

Mrs. Sears and Eleanora. I think Eleo is one of the most interesting figures in America. She has more charm than anybody I ever met and a devastating smile that Sargent caught so marvelously in his drawing of her. In the evenings at Beverly Farms when I had to stay indoors and play the piano for Mr. and Mrs. Sears, Eleo would be on the porch with a beau. I never knew anybody who had so many beaux and such nice ones, but she never married anybody. I loved Eleo and I still do. She calls me Birry. Every once in a while she'll wire to me: "Birry, where are you? Why don't you ever write? Why don't you come East? Love Eleo."

The Sears house in Beverly Farms was just down the street from Justice Holmes's. I was always thrilled to see him. I loved his loving detective stories; it was a great bond between us.

We reopened early and played and played and played all over the country. During the tour we went back to Philadelphia and for two weeks you couldn't get into the theater. We broke the record of the new Garrick Theatre in the same play and with the same cast that had met with such a cool reception two years before.

When one of the men of the company became suddenly ill, I telegraphed my brother Jack to come on and take his part. Jack had not been on the stage yet and took it all as a great joke. He had a very short part and was very funny in it. After the end of the second act, where I did the celebrated dance with a hysterical breaking-down at the end of it, there were always a great many curtain calls, when I took the whole company on the stage with me. When the curtains went up at the first curtain call on the first night of

Jack's appearance, much to my surprise Jack walked out from the crowd right to the footlights and bowed low—quite alone.

It was the silliest thing I have ever seen done, and, at the next curtain call, all of us were laughing hysterically at him. But he was not to be outdone; he graciously came forward, led me by the hand, bowed to me and then to the audience, as if he were introducing a shy debutante. It was not difficult then to realize that Jack would be a grand comedian.

When we closed in June, I was a star, with my name up in lights, but I was getting only $125 a week. Mr. Frohman said, "No matter what you get, Ethel, it'll go," and instead of a larger salary proposed that he give me a bonus, probably thinking that some of the bonus *wouldn't* go.

But instead of the bonus, I demanded that he give Lionel the part of the organ grinder in *The Mummy and the Humming Bird* in which Uncle Jack was to open in September. It was a wonderful part and I knew Lionel could play it superbly. Mr. Frohman had already decided on someone else, but I said, "Well, that's all I want and I really think Lionel should have it." And at last Mr. Frohman promised to let him do it.

When I went to England that summer, I took with me Berthe, the Swiss maid whom I had found through Kathleen Neilson. Berthe always loved being in England. I remember once her dashing into Mrs. Newhouse's sitting room in Claridge's and saying, "I'm having such a wonderful time!" and dashing right out again. She was to be with me for twenty years.

I had another lovely summer, staying with Millie Sutherland at Stafford House and with her sister Daisy at Warwick Castle and with Lady Randolph Churchill, Winston Churchill's mother. I kept seeing Winston there and everywhere, and the friendship that began between us then has lasted ever since.

He was in the House of Commons, and he and some other more or less unruly young members, Hugh Cecil, Lord Salisbury's son, and Ian Malcolm and others, were known as The Hooligans.

Winston and Henry James and Harry Rosslyn, Millie's brother, were at her cottage one weekend when I was there. At lunch Millie made the mistake of saying to Henry James, "Did you have a pleasant walk this morning?"

And he said, "Yes," in two and a half pages, with hardly a semicolon and never a period—a superb performance.

I saw Henry James quite often that summer and we got on tremendously well together. I loved to ask him questions and hear his long, rambling answers. My appearance always seemed to amuse him; he said I was rather Gothic and reminded him of a cornice on a Gothic building.

After that summer in London I did not see Henry James again for several years. Then one day, as I was walking along Fifth Avenue, a hansom stopped near me and suddenly someone jumped out almost at my feet, saying, "Hello." It was Henry James.

That summer in England when I was staying at Stafford House Edie Chaplin, who had married Charlie Castlereagh, was terribly ill with penumonia. I remember sitting up with her sister Florence in Edie's drawing room all through the night when the crisis was expected. The little room was filled with Charlie's brother officers in the Blues who, without taking time to change their uniforms after coming off duty, had come to sit and wait with Charlie. The sound of traffic in the street had been muffled by tanbark so that we sat in unusually somber silence until the crisis passed. It was a most extraordinary night.

Charlie's name always reminded me of the Congress of Vienna in which another Lord Castlereagh played such an important part.

Peter Pan was playing in London with Pauline Chase as Peter, her first part, although she had been in several musical comedies, and with Gerald du Maurier as both Captain Hook and Mr. Darling. I was in Mr. Frohman's office at the Savoy Hotel when he and Barrie were deciding to take the play to Paris for one performance. Barrie said, "Why not take little Ethel along with us?"

And they did. It was the first time I had ever been to Paris, but I paid almost no attention to it; I was too excited about being with the company and seeing the play.

In London I saw *A Country Mouse,* a light satiric comedy which was to be my next play. I bought lovely new white clothes for it from Madame Hayward. They were all white, which was part of the satire.

Then I went to Dunrobin in August, stayed again with Margot and Henry Asquith on my way down to London, and then came back to New York.

The Mummy and the Humming Bird had opened early in September, and Lionel, as I had been sure he would, was making an enormous impression as the organ grinder. Florence and John Magee asked me to go with them to see the play. They were taking an Italian count, a Roman, with them, and I asked Florence to put me next to him because I wanted to see what effect Lionel's performance—he didn't speak a word of English in the part—would have on a real Italian.

In the play Uncle Jack was supposed to be a gentleman expecting a lady to dinner in his rooms in London. There was a beautiful table ready for her but she was late, and finally, when he realized that she wasn't coming, he angrily told his servant to go out to the street and bring in the first person that he saw, man or woman. The servant brought in Lionel with his organ and his monkey. With neither Uncle Jack nor Lionel supposed to speak or understand a word of the other's language, the scene between them was terrific and Lionel was simply superb in it.

After the first act I turned to the count and said, "What did you think of the Italian?"

He said indignantly, "He is *not* an Italian. He is a Sicilian."

Probably the best notice anyone ever got!

❧ IV ❧

This Time There Was
No Escape

It was while I was playing in Washington in *A Country Mouse* that Theodore Roosevelt amazed me by his extraordinary memory. Alice Roosevelt was a friend of mine, and she had asked me to lunch at the White House, where I sat next to Mr. Roosevelt. He had seen the play the night before, and seemed to know it as well as I did. He quoted speech after speech from it, absolutely verbatim.

Alice and I were going to the matinee at Keith's after lunch with Nick Longworth and Marguerite Cassini, and when Alice went upstairs to put on her hat I went with her. The White House elevator in those days was an old-fashioned, self-service one, operated by a rope. Quentin and Kermit, Alice's little half-brothers, thought it would be funny to open the doors so the elevator couldn't move. They kept us between floors for over an hour while they roared with laughter. We could not make anybody hear us.

During all this time Nick was downstairs with Marguerite Cassini, one of the most attractive girls in Washington. Alice was not amused. Almost immediately afterward she and Nick were engaged. Alice was and is brilliant, attractive, arresting. Her marriage to Nick Longworth was the marriage of two of my very dearest friends.

I visited her many times and I shall never forget the little Roosevelts dashing around the lower floor of the White House on roller skates. When I read Mr. Roosevelt's *Letters to His Children* it did not surprise me at all to learn that they had pillow fights on the upper floors.

Some years ago, about three presidential elections back, I

was in Washington again and a newspaperman asked me whom I was for in the election, Roosevelt or Dewey. I never had liked Mr. Dewey very much, and I said, "Roosevelt." So, for lack of news, I suppose, they printed it in the newspapers.

As I walked into my room, back at the hotel, the telephone was ringing. I went to it, picked up the receiver, and the voice said, "Traitor!"

I said, "Hello, Alice."

"How dare you!"

I said, "Come over here and don't be silly."

She was over there in about two minutes. The close friendship between us has always continued, in spite of some differences of opinion. Whenever I was playing in Washington I used to go with Alice practically every day and sit in the Senate gallery and listen to the debate.

The year that I played *A Country Mouse* in New York I lived in the first place I had ever been able to call my own. It was an apartment on West Fifty-ninth Street, overlooking the park—a place I love to remember. There were eight rooms and the rent was $100 a month. Years later I had another apartment in the same building, on Central Park South, three doors down from the Plaza, with three rooms for $300 a month.

I remember that I had a wonderful time buying the furniture, especially the piano which was the first of the series of Steinways I have owned and loved. Already I had a lot of books and a really considerable collection of music. There was a music room opening off from the living room. I bought a "Winged Victory" and hung copies of my favorite paintings on the walls—"The Pearl Diver" which I had seen in the Louvre, and some of Whistler's. The walls of the apartment were white and I had a dark red sofa. I remember wanting a gold-colored one because Mummum had had a dull gold brocade sofa in her house and my mother had had one in London but I couldn't afford it or the kind of furniture to go with it.

In those days, as I began to be well known, girls of my own age or near it began dressing like me, imitating my hats and the way I wore my hair. This was a surprise to me; I had not been aware of it until reporters began writing that it had become a prevailing fashion. My hair was straight, so I wore it that way. It was brown, so I wore it brown, simply arranged—just as it is now except that it has been cut and then it was in a knot, low at the back.

During all those years when it had been necessary for me to count the pennies that I spent on clothes I had decided that the cheapest way to dress, both inexpensively and well, was to wear black or white or gray. So I wore black or white or gray, and kept on doing it more or less long after expense had ceased to be so important.

I had some other ideas about dress and still have them, the same ideas. I would say to an interviewer today very much the same things that I said to Gustav Kobbé when he came to interview me in that apartment on Central Park South. In the *Ladies' Home Journal* for June, 1903, he quoted me— accurately—as saying:

It is the way a dress is cut and made and worn that makes it pretty. The material doesn't matter much. Put good work into the most ordinary material and you have a pretty dress. I once had a dress made of hopsacking—just the rough, common kind. I had it well made and well cut, and it was as much admired as any dress I ever had. Take this red corduroy I have on now. I could just as well have had it of red velvet. It would have cost much more. But I preferred it of corduroy; first, because it cost less, and second because I like to take an inexpensive material and make something pretty out of it.

It is just as easy to dress well as it is to dress badly if a girl will only be simple. It isn't always easy to get a dress simple, I know, but when you do, just see what you have; the most artistic thing you can get in the way of a gown. I hate conspicuousness in dress. I know lots of girls who would look perfectly charming if their dresses were more simply made. But they put a lot of fussy things on them and they spoil their dresses and their own looks. For no girl ever looks well in a fussy dress—at least none of the girls that I know and I know lots. On the other hand, a perfectly simple dress, well made, always makes a good-looking girl the more charming, and makes a homely girl look better.

I had to make my own clothes long enough to learn something about dressmaking, and when I could afford to have a dressmaker make them for me, I was able to tell her what I wanted and just how it was to be built. I had begun to design, not only my own dresses, but those I wore on the stage, and it had been my idea that white dresses would give satiric point to the assumed simplicity of the masquerading girl in *A Country Mouse*. But the white dresses that Madame Hayward made in London at my suggestion not only pointed that satire; the photographs of them prove, I think, the soundness of my youthful faith in simplicity and in black and white. Nobody seemed to think they were unfashionable or conspicuous when I first wore them; they would have been—and were—"in style" in any one of the fifty years since they were new, and they would be perfectly in style now. I have never made any compromise with fashions, no matter how extreme they were.

When I was becoming affluent I could afford to have my dresses made by Mrs. Osborne. She was a lady—I don't know how else to describe her than to say that—who had decided, when she needed money, to become a dressmaker in a small way. That was before the days when "ladies" went in for such things as dressmaking, interior decorating and so on. But Mrs. Osborne became *the* dressmaker of New York. The white dress that I wore in the photograph in which I have oak leaves in my hair was one of hers.

Once in Paris she took me to a dressmakers' showing of clothes at Paquin's. I was wearing one of Mrs. Osborne's dresses. Madame Paquin came across the room and said, "Madame, that is the most beautiful dress I have ever seen."

I smiled and pointed to Mrs. Osborne and Madame Paquin congratulated her.

While I was furnishing the apartment I began rehearsing in *A Country Mouse,* in which, for the first time, Bruce McRae was my leading man.

I could always see and hear everything that happened in the audience. Fortunately nobody knew that I could. Soon after we opened *A Country Mouse* at the Savoy Theatre— the Savoy was very long and narrow, like the early movie theaters—I saw a man come down the aisle and speak to a woman. She got up and went with him to the lobby. Just as they reached the door, I saw her throw up her arms and fall

SAVOY THEATRE.

CHARLES FROHMAN, • • • • • MANAGER.
Also Manager of the Empire, Criterion, Garrick, Madison Square and Garden Theatres, New York City, and DUKE OF YORK'S and VAUDEVILLE THEATRES, LONDON, ENG.

Evenings at 8.10.   Matinees Wednesday and Saturday at 2.

EXTRA MATINEE ELECTION DAY.

CHARLES FROHMAN Presents
ETHEL BARRYMORE
IN THE COMEDY, IN THREE ACTS, ENTITLED
A COUNTRY MOUSE
By ARTHUR LAW.
As Played at the Prince of Wales Theatre and Criterion Theatre, London.

CAST.

DUKE OF ST. KITS...HARRY DAVENPORT
LORD ROBERT WYCKHAM..............................GEORGE W. HOWARD
HON. ARCHIBALD VYSE.................................BRUCE McRAE
JOHN BOWLBY, M. P....................................ARTHUR ELLIOT
JEPH OT, a butler.......................................JAMES KEARNEY
FOOTMAN.. ....HUGO GOLDSMITH
LADY SYLVIA BOWLBY.... . ...ADELAIDE PRINCE
VIOLET AYNSLEY ....MAY LAMBERT
MRS. CROPPER............ ....MRS. FANNY ADDISON PITT
ANGELA MUIR............. ....ETHEL BARRYMORE

ACT I.—Drawing Room in Lady Sylvia Bowlby's House in Park Lane.
Evening.
ACT II.—Morning Room in Mr. Aynsley's House in Kensington.
The following morning.
ACT III.—Hon. Archibald Vyse's Chambers in Bond Street.
The same afternoon.

PRECEDED BY
CARROTS
A STUDY, IN ONE ACT, By JULES RENARD.
Translated by ALFRED SUTRO.
(As presented at the Theatre Antoine, Paris.)

MR. LEPIC...BRUCE McREA
MRS LEPIC............. ....MRS. FANNY ADDISON PITT
C RROTS, their son..ETHEL BARRYMORE
ANNETTE.......... ....BEATRICE AGNEW

Produced under the stage direction of JOSEPH HUMPHREYS.
Scenery by E. G. UNITT.

Programme continued on second page following.

on her face. When the curtain went down, I asked the manager what had happened.

At first he pretended that he didn't know what I meant,
but I said, "What happened to that woman? I saw her fall."

Then he told me that her husband had just been killed in
a terrible wreck in the Grand Central tunnel.

The play was a success in New York and on tour. When
we were in Boston I got a letter saying, "Would it be possible
to give me an hour or maybe two? I would like to do a drawing of you and I would be so honored to present you with
the drawing afterward." The letter was signed John Singer
Sargent.

Of course it was the most exciting thing. He was working
on his "Prophets" for the Boston Public Library at the time
and was staying with the Montgomery Searses. Mrs. Sears
had given him the whole top floor of her house for his studio,
and that is where he made the sketch of me. I remember
that he always had trouble with the self-working elevator. It
would stop and go, stop and go, and finally get there.

He was delightful, humming around the room while he
worked. He would sit down occasionally while in the midst
of the drawing and play little snatches on the piano and then
come back to his work again. He found it was very hard to
draw my mouth. He would say, "I try to draw a delicate line
and I produce a beam."

He gave me the drawing which he said later was his
favorite charcoal. It is quite my most treasured possession.

It was during this season that I saw my father on the stage
for the last time. I can remember having seen him in only

two plays. Once, when I was quite small, I was taken to see him as Armand in *The Lady of the Camellias* with Olga Nethersole. What I remember best about that is after the play he took me to Miss Nethersole's dressing room where she terrified me by asking me to recite something for her. The only other play in which I can remember having seen him was the last one in which he ever appeared. He was superb as Rawdon Crawley in *Becky Sharp* with Mrs. Fiske.

I have always regretted that I saw so little of him. I remember his superlative beauty and how engaging and gay he was, but I heard all the amusing anecdotes about him and his stabbing wit only from other people. Even so, though, it is good to remember them. One of them that I like best is the story of the pompous man who kept saying, "I'm a self-made man. Sir, sir, absolutely self-made."

And my father said, "What interrupted you?"

And another that I love to remember is the one about the dramatic critic on the *Police Gazette*, a pink paper that was read only in barbershops. The critic had written something offensive about father and the next time they met he said, "Did you see what I wrote about you, Barrymore?"

And father said, "No. I shave myself."

Father wrote a dramatization of *Les Misérables* and wanted to play Jean Valjean in it. Someone said to him, "But, Barry, can you get a New York manager to produce it?"

"Produce it?" Father said. "I can't get a New York manager to pronounce it!"

He hated and resented the second-rate Englishmen who came over here. One night one of them who had just arrived turned up at the Lambs Club a little tight and began to talk about the harbor that he had just sailed into.

"Why the British Fleet could come in and take it in half an hour."

Father said, "What, again?"

But in the best of all the stories about him it is my mother who carried off the honors. One Sunday morning as she was leaving the house on her way to church, she met my father on the doorstep just coming in. He was still in evening clothes, top hat, white tie and tails, buttonhole, very jaunty. He said, "Well, Georgie, where are you going?"

And she said, "I am going to mass and you can go to hell."

A really proper convert!

Father wrote a play called *Nadjezda* and sent it to Sarah Bernhardt in Paris. Two years later *Tosca* was produced and it was practically father's play even down to the candles. Bernhardt dismissed his protests. Nothing was ever done about the theft of his play. He never got over it. When he was dying, he still talked about it.

Father's friend, Tyrone Power, played *Nadjezda* in Australia and it was also played in London.

Sometimes when father was in Philadelphia, he would come to the convent and take me out to lunch, but he could never take me to his hotel because he always lived in terrible ones. He had to, because he always traveled with his animals —a mongoose, a raccoon and some monkeys and birds—and had to go to some hotel that would take in his menagerie.

I shall always wish that I might have seen him oftener and known him better.

As soon as the season in *A Country Mouse* closed I fled

again to London. I felt as though I had not left it for an hour. Life was very full and very interesting. In all the years that I went back, none of my friends—who became most intimate friends—ever took my theatrical life seriously. They thought I was on the stage for a pastime—if at all. When any of them came to America, they were surprised to find that I was more or less prominent.

My London friends were real friends. When I returned from America they always acted as if I had just been to the country for a weekend and it made me feel as if it were really true.

There were marvelous balls at Stafford House. I remember Millie standing at the top of the stairs, receiving King Edward and Queen Alexandra. All the men were in uniform, wearing decorations, and the colors of it all were unforgettably beautiful.

And I remember being with Mrs. Samuel Newhouse in her box at the first night of *Madame Butterfly*—its first performance anywhere—with Emmy Destinn, and Caruso and Scotti, and in the royal box was Queen Alexandra with her lovely little head.

Everybody loved Mrs. Newhouse. King Edward said she was the "nicest little American woman who ever came to London." She never had a big house. She lived first at Claridge's and then at the Ritz and gave dinners downstairs.

Samuel Newhouse was enormously rich but later lost his fortune. After his death Mrs. Newhouse went to California and lived in one room at the Beverly Hills Hotel, making her own clothes instead of buying them at Worth's, making her own hats instead of getting them from Reboux, wearing imitation pearls instead of the terrific string of real ones that she had once owned, but looking as smart as ever, and nobody ever heard her say a word of bitterness. Today, just before I wrote these words, I sent her a telegram wishing her a happy birthday—her ninetieth.

I went to a ball at Grosvenor House, given for the Crown Prince and Princess of Rumania. What I noticed about the Crown Princess was that, unlike most of the princesses I had seen, she was very smart and beautifully dressed. I was wandering about when a tall, golden-haired, absolutely beautiful young man came up to me and said, "What are you looking for, little girl?"

I said, "I'm looking for 'The Blue Boy.'"

He said, "Come with me," and took me down a long hall to a library, a small room in relation to the size of the house, and there over the fireplace was "Blue Boy."

He was the Duke of Westminster and that was his house.

In August I came back to New York to begin rehearsing my new play, *Cousin Kate,* a light comedy by Hubert Henry Davies that I had seen in England.

Weber and Fields had Tuesday matinees so that I could go to see them every week. They put on a perfectly wonderful show—this is one time when that word is exactly right —in which they always had a terrifically funny take-off on some current success. I was thrilled when they did not only *Captain Jinks* but *Carrots,* too, with Fay Templeton playing me. In their company were people like Lillian Russell and Peter Daly, and Willie Collier and May Irwin and David Warfield and many others who were or became famous in their own right. They even had Charles Belmont Davis as manager, all dressed up every night in white tie and tails, making a magnificent front and enjoying himself immensely.

What I remember best about the tour of *Cousin Kate* was something that happened when we were playing in Boston. Sir Henry Irving was there making his final tour of America, by himself, without Ellen Terry. He was playing *Louis XI*. I had never seen it and I very much wanted to see him die in it so one night I dashed over to the stage door of the Colonial Theatre, and they smuggled me in. I hid behind the black velvet curtains and watched Sir Henry die on a stone bench. The curtain stayed down as it always did when he died on the stage. And he looked up under his eyebrows and said, "Is that the little Bullfinch there?"

I went over and sat on the bench with him. He said, "And so you're a great star now."

I said, "Oh no, Sir Henry. That's the system here."

"What's the matter?" he said. "Aren't you happy?"

"No, not very," I said.

"What do they say about you?" he said.

"Oh, they say I look all right and I have this and that and the other, but that I am always Ethel Barrymore."

He put his long, delicate hand on mine and said, "See to it that they never say anything else."

Those words have carried me through all the years. No notice ever made me miserable again.

The next summer when I went back to London I took an apartment in Charles Street in Berkeley Square and Jack spent part of the summer with me there.

Sommie Somerset, who was one of the "Three Gringos" in Dick Davis's book, was married to Lady Katherine Beauclerk, daughter of the Duke of St. Albans, direct descendant of Charles II and Nell Gwyn. Kitty thought it would be fun if she and Sommie and Jack and I all went off and took rooms at an inn somewhere without any maids or valets. So we all went to a small place on the river where we took all the rooms they had. When Sommie, Jack and I went down to dinner, there was no Kitty and after we had waited a long time for her, I went upstairs and found her sitting before a dressing table crying. She said, "I don't know how to put up my hair."

I put it up for her and we went downstairs.

Consuelo Vanderbilt Balsan's book says that Kitty resembled her Stuart ancestors, but to me she looked amazingly like some of the portraits of Nell Gwyn.

While I was in England that summer I had a very funny experience, staying at Warwick Castle with a large house party. I had been there several times before but this time I was given a huge, magnificent room, the kind of a room you look at and say, "Queen Elizabeth must have slept here." I think Daisy gave it to me because there was a bathroom down the hall, a real bathroom. I had put on a dressing gown, screwed my hair up tight on top of my head and, with a sponge in my hand, started down the famous corridor for the bathroom. Turning a corner, I walked straight into a group of American tourists (the castle was open to the public every Thursday, though I didn't know it). Just as I was flying by, I heard a girl say, "Why, Mamma! That was Ethel Barrymore!" What a confusing and startling experience for people who had expected to see the ghost of Queen Elizabeth at least.

Another thing I remember that year was Anthony and

Betty Hope giving a dinner for Millie Sutherland, for which they had hired a very, very ancient butler. They coached him patiently to announce "Her Grace, the Duchess of Sutherland" but when the time came he was tongue-tied, so Millie came in, giggling, and announced herself.

I was always trying to let myself get married. There was a friend of many friends of mine named Harry Graham, a gay, brilliant creature of great charm and attraction who had written several books of verse. He liked me, too, and there I was again with a faint hope that this time was it.

His family were extremely kind to me. They lived in the House of Lords end of the Houses of Parliament. His father, Sir Henry Graham, held some legal position in the House of Lords. The first time I met him I saw him come hurrying through the Gothic halls leading from the House of Lords to his own domicile to be in time for tea to meet Harry's young lady. He had on a full-bottomed wig, slightly askew, and a flowing gown. Whenever I dined there, Sir Henry would go to the piano and sing comic songs, of which he had an enormous repertory. Something about him always touched me very deeply.

I kept on meeting Harry at the different country houses where I stayed and also in London. Once we were both staying with the Lucases in their thatched cottage. They had just a little ground but you could see meadows and fields as far as the horizon. We used to sit on the grass singing symphonies, trying to outdo each other in remembering them. It was great fun.

When James Barrie had a cricket week—artists versus writers—Harry was there as an author, along with many others. Some of us stayed at Barrie's house and the overflow stayed at an inn. We all ate at the house—in the garden, in the sitting room and in the dining room. There were a great many of us: Edwin Abbey in white flannels, rather fat, dashing around catching cricket balls, or rather not catching them; and Maurice Hewlett, playing cricket rather romantically. And, of course, Barrie himself. It was a wonderful party. After cricket when we came back to the house Barrie used to play croquet on the lawn. Little Michael Davies, the grandson of George du Maurier, never left Barrie's side. He was about four or five years old. Barrie, with his pipe in his mouth, holding a croquet mallet in one hand and the other clasping the little boy's hand, would walk quietly all over the lawn. The little fellow never left him, and he never left the little boy if he could help it.

Millie Sutherland knew that I was staying at Barrie's house and was quite envious. She loved literary people and was always trying to meet them. She sent me a note, saying that she was passing through, and I asked Barrie if she could stop for tea. She did and stayed for dinner.

Once when Harry was at tea with Jack and me in the apartment in Charles Street, Edgar Wace, our cousin who was in the Civil Service, stopped in to say good-by on his way to a new job in Egypt.

Edgar for some reason talked like a musical-comedy Englishman, quite unreal and enormously exaggerated, and when he left, Captain Harry Graham, D.S.O., of the Cold Stream Guards, said, twinkling, "That, I suppose, is what would be called an English accent."

One of Harry's cousins was the Duchess of Portland. She

was very beautiful. She wore huge, pale pink carnations called "Malmaisons" that came from her greenhouses. The Duke was Master of Horse for King Edward. We went to lunch there one day, and I was delighted and charmed by the tall, powdered-haired footmen in their scarlet coats. Apparently anyone connected with the royal household dressed his footmen in scarlet coats. Perhaps an English girl would have taken it as a matter of course, but it was rather like a fairy tale to me.

I had hoped that I would be able to bring myself to marry Harry Graham and so did all of our friends. I remember when I came back to America again I had quite a row with Helen Hay, who was very angry with me because I hadn't gone through with it. But although I really agonized about it because it was a fine and rare human being that I was hurting, I knew I might have hurt him more if I married him without being far surer of myself than I was. I will always be glad that we remained friends all our lives.

I want to make it quite clear that I have written about having been engaged to Harry and to Laurence Irving and Gerald du Maurier only because so much has been written, often so inaccurately, about these three engagements. Growing up, as I did, in a household where personal affairs were never spoken of—much less discussed—made this goldfish-bowl existence a horror for me. Of course there were no columnists then, but I hated people peering. I had practically two lives, side by side, the theater and the other, my private life, which doesn't exist any more but which I, for many years, clung to.

The goldfish bowl has been one of the hardest things I

have had to cope with. It is growing, or the vulgarity of it seems to be growing, and it is not limited to the theater; it goes, apparently, with making a mark of any kind. Nowadays there are paid publicists; I gladly would have paid *not* to be written about.

Back home to America in September again for work. I was successful enough now to be sure that Mr. Frohman would always have a play waiting for me, and this year it was *Sunday*.

I had to invent an accent for "Sunday." In the play I was a foundling who had been brought up by four miners, three of them old, one young, who all talked like Bret Harte characters, so I talked like that, too, with hard "r's" and my own idea of a broad frontier accent. Before my first entrance, when one of the miners called to me to know where something was, I answered from offstage, "It's on the bew-rah." There was a very distinguished old critic, William Winter, who said I was particularly good in this play because it suited my form of speech!

In the second act, which took place in England, I read aloud to my English relatives a letter from the "boys" who had brought me up. I came to a part that I didn't want them to hear, and I stopped and my aunt said, "Go on, Sunday."

According to the script I just ran off the stage without answering, so at one of the early rehearsals I said to Mr. Frohman, who was sitting down in the orchestra, "It seems so rude just to run off without saying anything. I think I ought to say something to her."

He said rather testily, "Well, well, what do you want to say?"

I said, "Oh, maybe something like 'That's all there is. There isn't any more.'"

For some reason that line has been given an importance far beyond its merit or its meaning. It was just thrown in to get me off the stage politely. It meant nothing; it had nothing to do with anything. But it has become a universal saying, given many different meanings, some of them deep, some of them sinister—gangsters use it just before they pull the trigger and there's a current play that ends with it.

I had forgotten all about its origin until one time when I had promised to do something in an Actors' Fund benefit and finally decided to do an imitation of Cissie Loftus and Elsie Janis imitating me. Cissie Loftus always imitated me reading the letter from *Sunday*, and I went to Mr. Frohman's office, where the bound manuscripts of all the plays that he ever produced were on file, to copy the passage that I needed. But when Mr. Reilly, who was in charge, let me see the manuscript of *Sunday* that passage wasn't there, and then suddenly I remembered how I had made it up at that rehearsal.

It had never even been typed into the manuscript of the play!

One reason why *Sunday* was fun to do was because it was a character performance, because it wasn't me. Character parts are wonderful things for actors to hide behind. *Sunday* seldom got good notices because all the critics knew it had been written by four actors and that damned it in their eyes. But the public, undaunted, came to it in droves.

And I wonder what would happen to a play that was written by four critics.

People who saw it only once were able to quote from it years afterward. I think it was in this play that I began to realize for the first time that the stage was where I belonged, that this was going to be my life.

It was while I was playing *Sunday* in Philadelphia that Alf Hayman came over to tell me that my father had died.

We closed the play for a few nights. Mr. Hayman brought me back to New York, where I met Jack. He and I telegraphed Uncle Jack to ask if we might bury father in the Drew family plot in Philadelphia and he said we might. So we brought father back to Philadelphia, and only Jack and I and some old family retainers we hadn't seen for years were at the cemetery. This ended a chapter in my life that has always seemed tragically incomplete.

When we reopened the play Jack joined the company and played the young miner, Jacky, for the rest of the long tour. He was awfully good sometimes, when he wanted to be, but he was not taking the theater very seriously then.

On that tour we had quite a little trouble with Jack, and several times I had to telephone Mr. Frohman to telegraph Jack that he was fired. Then Jack, who hadn't been speaking to me for days, would come and say, "Here's a telegram from Charles Frohman. You've got to do something about it." And I would say, "You've got to pull yourself together," and he'd say, "I will. I will." And here and there he did.

While we were in San Francisco, Ashton Stevens and a detective took Jack and me all through Chinatown. That was before the earthquake, and we saw the fascinating, old Chinatown that nobody will ever see again.

After the tour was over, someone persuaded me to do a matinee of *A Doll's House* in Boston. Jack was staying in Maine, but I got him down to play Dr. Rank. He didn't want to do it, but I made him. That was when I knew he was always going to be good, and more than good. This was even before he attempted the light comedy parts in which he was so successful, like *The Fortune Hunter* and *Kick In*. People thought they discovered him when he played in *Justice* but I discovered him long before in *Sunday* and in *A Doll's House*.

At the end of the season of *Sunday* I went back to London. *Alice-Sit-by-the-Fire* was playing there with Ellen Terry taking the mother's part and Irene Vanbrugh in the part of the daughter. I went to see the play and a little one-act piece which preceded it—*Pantaloon* also by Barrie and played by Gerald du Maurier.

This one-act play had so devastated me and made me cry so hard that I could not go that night to see *Alice-Sit-by-the-Fire* all by itself, without seeing *Pantaloon* first.

Of course Mr. Frohman had these plays for America and he wanted me to take the part of the daughter in *Alice*, as I was then about twenty-one years of age. But, greatly to his and my surprise, Barrie insisted that I play the part of the mother. I could not understand why Mr. Barrie wanted me to play this part, so I asked him.

He said, "Because I see you playing it and hear you saying all those things in the last act."

Barrie said that I had "the mother thing" and he had his

way. I had white in my hair and wore long earrings and tried to believe that I looked forty, but the other day I saw a photograph of me in the part and I didn't look forty; I looked eight. Apparently, though, it was all right. The play was a success.

I remember how Barrie and Mr. Frohman used to sit together hour after hour in Mr. Frohman's rooms in the Savoy Hotel in London, sometimes talking and sometimes not uttering a sound for, oh, spaces of time. Often I would be with them and would wonder what they were thinking about, if anything—Barrie eating his little pipe and Mr. Frohman smoking many cigars, and not saying a word.

One day after Barrie had gone Mr. Frohman said, "Wasn't he wonderful? What do you suppose he was thinking about?"

I was still pretty young and I said, "I don't suppose he was thinking about anything."

Mr. Frohman didn't like that.

I spent a weekend with Lord and Lady Railey. Lord Railey was a great scientist, and there was another younger scientist there named Ray Lankester. I remember that after dinner he took me out into the garden and put a big glove on his hand. There was something on it that looked like a piece of coal with a spot in it that shone brightly. "That's radium," he told me.

In September I came back to New York to begin rehearsals in *Alice-Sit-by-the-Fire*.

Jack had a part in *Alice-Sit-by-the-Fire* and also appeared with Lionel in *Pantaloon*, so that when we opened at the Criterion, all three of us were at least in the same theater, which was the nearest we ever came to being in the same play. Lionel was superb as Pantaloon and so was Jack as Harlequin. He would leap across the room and land cross-legged on a table, although he had never done it before.

It was during this season that Lionel got a nervous terror of the theater and became almost obsessed with the idea that he was going to forget his lines. He never did forget them, but the fear was so strong in him that he came to me one day and said he could not go on—that he must stop. He did stop acting for several years and went to live in Paris to study painting, but eventually, I am glad to say, he came back to the theater, where he belonged. He was only a fairly good artist but a really great actor, so I was very happy when he came back to his own field, in which I have always felt he was superb.

Tommy Kelly played the part of my ensign son, about sixteen, and at the end of the play, he and I and Bruce McRae, who played the father, and the girl who played the daughter were all on the stage together in fond embrace. One night in Boston Tommy didn't appear, and the curtain came down without him. It turned out that he had somehow thought the play was over and gone home. When I sent for him, he was very contrite.

He said, "I don't know why I ever did it, but it won't ever happen again."

Well, it did happen again in about two weeks. I had him come to my dressing room and I said, "Tommy, this is awful. I don't know what we are going to do about you."

He said, "I have a brother who looks just like me and if we had him here, he could take my place in case I should ever forget again."

That was how Gregory Kelly came to us. We kept him with us as insurance all the way out to California. I kept waiting for a night when both Tommy and Gregory would be missing but neither of them ever was.

We were scheduled to end our tour in the spring with two weeks in Boston, but Jack decided to go to Australia with Willie Collier in *The Dictator* and so I arranged with Uncle Googan to take his place in the play in Boston, but Uncle Googan never got a chance to play the part. I was suddenly stricken with appendicitis and the Boston engagement had to be canceled.

Jack said good-by to me in the hospital and departed for San Francisco, where, having come in late from a dance, he was lying on top of his bed in his hotel room in full evening dress with a flower in his buttonhole when the earthquake threw him into the bathroom.

He managed to get down to the street and decided to try to get to the Tobins' at Burlingame, but on the way the army got him and put a shovel in his hand and said dig. This called forth Uncle Jack's famous remark that it took a convulsion of nature to make Jack take a bath and the United States Army to put him to work.

When I left the hospital I took a cottage at Cornish, New Hampshire, a place of beautiful gardens where many artists and authors lived. To me the most exciting of them was Saint-Gaudens. He was then doing his wonderful Lincoln, and he used to let me watch him work. The head was finished, and I never could look at it without wanting to cry. Saint-Gaudens was very ill that summer—in fact, he was dying. I have always felt it a great privilege to have known him at all.

My house belonged to the Harry Fullers, she being Lucia Fairchild, who painted such beautiful miniatures. It was a most charming place with a swimming pool in the garden, surrounded by a brick wall, and I had an enormous studio. Richard Harding Davis and his wife came to stay with me, and also my friend, Mrs. Wolcott, from Buffalo.

Kenyon Cox made a painting of my head that summer for a figure of *Justice* which he was painting for the Newark, New Jersey, courthouse. I was fascinated by his enormous studio, and by his climbing up on ladders to do his huge canvases. I had never seen anyone doing a big mural before.

I liked Percy MacKaye very much that summer, and also the Jesse Lynch Williamses and their children. All the children did *The Rose and the Ring* and of course I helped. They were charming. I cannot remember all the different children's names, but I do remember little Clara Fuller, who was splendid, and so was little Ruth Hapgood. William Vaughan Moody read me the original version of *The Great Divide* and Harry Fuller did a charming drawing of me that summer. Mrs. Houston, Charlotte Fairchild's mother, who had a house at Cornish, also painted me.

I also saw much of Maxfield Parrish and his father, Stephen Parrish that summer. The latter had one of the most beautiful gardens I have ever seen—even more beautiful than the Charles Platts' and the Norman Hapgoods', which is saying a great deal. It was a most interesting summer.

I went over to Dublin, New Hampshire, which is about fifty miles from Cornish, to visit Joseph Smith, the artist. They were having some kind of garden fete and I was to be a sprite coming up from a fountain. Mark Twain was one of the guests that night. He was always very nice to me. It was the first time I had seen him in white evening clothes. I met him with Bob Collier at dinner in New York shortly afterward, and he was still in his white evening clothes. I saw him again at some big benefit at an opera house where there were booths. He was sitting in the book stall, signing things, when I passed by. He called out, "Oh, there's the water sprite!"

I remember, too, Mrs. Winston Churchill, the wife of the American Winston Churchill, the novelist, asking me if I would drive her beautiful horses in the horse show. I had never driven at all, but I had seen a lot of horse shows and driven with good drivers, especially Eleo Sears, who was a superb one. I knew how to hold the reins, so without thinking, I said yes and won the blue ribbon. How extraordinarily cheeky I must have been!

That winter I went on tour with *Alice-Sit-by-the-Fire* and I think it was the following spring that Mr. Frohman took me to London to play in a piece by Hubert Henry Davies called *Cynthia*. I remember being very terrified and wishing that I had not done it.

The Anthony Hopes gave me a supper party after *Cynthia*. The play was not a success. So, after playing about six weeks, I went to Scotland, made some visits and then, with Mr. and Mrs. Ben Webster, Mr. and Mrs. H. V. Esmond, Gerald du Maurier, Anthony Hope and Cecelia Loftus, I went for a summer holiday to a small place in County Kerry, Ireland. There was nothing there at all except an inn and a few little huts—real huts, with pigs and old women with pipes. The young Irish girls we met were most amazingly beautiful; as you passed them they would look up with eyelashes that seemed to sweep the dust, blue eyes and oval faces. Terrific poverty but terrific beauty!

One of our party, Cecelia Loftus, was a real genius as a mimic. There was something very touching about that poignant personality—no one else has ever been like her. She was most kind and generous and would give anybody anything she had.

We occupied the entire inn, it was so small, just as if it were our own country house. We had a marvelous time, fishing and swimming. It was in the bicycle days, and we used to ride along a beautiful road at the edge of a cliff right above the sea, just as the sun was setting back of the mountains. One day I was bicycling along this road alone when suddenly I heard the most unearthly sounds, that seemed to come from the mountains just above me. Finally I saw figures covered with shawls and bent over, moving along above me. They were on their way to a wake and, as they walked over the mountains, they kept up a continual "keening." It was most unearthly.

That fall in New York I played in *The Silver Box,* the first Galsworthy play to be produced in America. I played the part of Mrs. Jones, a tragic figure—a beautiful part and a magnificent play. What I suppose I may call my public was aghast at my appearing as a charwoman in rags, so it did not succeed financially. While I was doing the play, I had some charming letters and cables from Mr. Galsworthy but, much to my regret, I never met him.

During the run of *The Silver Box* when I was living on

West Fortieth Street, a friend of mine, Chloese Hatch, asked me to come out to Tuxedo for lunch on Sunday. I discovered that there was practically no way to get to Tuxedo except in a car, so I decided to hire one for the day. On Saturday evening Chloese called me up and said a man was coming down for lunch, too, and his car had broken down. Would I stop for him and bring him down and back? So I did. After lunch he wandered off into the woods with a very pretty girl, and they came back engaged. Everybody was very pleased about it. I drove him back, deposited him at his door and went on my way.

He turned out to be George Baker, one of the richest men in the world. It always struck me as ridiculous that I should be the one who paid for the automobile.

Tuxedo in winter looked like a Currier and Ives painting with the lake frozen over and children skating on it.

When *The Silver Box* closed, I went on tour in a revival of *Captain Jinks*. When we got to Boise, Idaho, early one morning, there was a very strange atmosphere in the hotel lobby. It was full of extraordinary-looking people and everybody seemed to be armed. A big man came over to me and asked me if I was Ethel Barrymore, and when I said yes, he said, "I was a great friend of your father's. My name is McFarland. I'm a Pinkerton man."

I said, "What's happening here?"

"Don't you know? This is the Haywood trial. The whole town is a fort."

He took me into a room upstairs and lifted up the mattress. There were Winchesters under it. He said there were rifles under every mattress in the hotel.

I knew a girl, a friend of Ruth Hanna's and Alice Roosevelt's named Margaret Cobb, whose father owned the paper in Boise City. I went to lunch in their lovely house, and when I said I was interested in the trial, Mr. Cobb said, "Would you like to go to it?"

And I said, "I would, very much."

Harry Orchard, the killer, was on the stand. A man named Clarence Darrow was counsel for Haywood and a man named William Borah was the district attorney. There was a dreamy-looking man sitting next to me; his name was Gifford Pinchot.

Orchard on the stand looked like a respectable grocer; a little like Mr. Hobbs in *Little Lord Fauntleroy*. He confessed to twenty-six murders! He said he had been employed by Haywood over a period of years to kill mining bosses. The jury were the most wonderful-looking men I've ever seen. They were all ranchers with the bluest eyes, like sailors' eyes, used to looking at great distances. They made me think of Uncle Sam as Uncle Sam ought to look without the goatee. They were magnificent, all of them, but the only evidence against Haywood was the testimony of a confessed murderer, and there was nothing they could do but let Haywood go free.

That was the first I had heard of the flowery Mr. Darrow. He had all the props, an old mother in a wheelchair and a little girl with curls draped around Haywood. I don't know whether she was his daughter or just one of Mr. Darrow's props.

Afterward I said to Mr. Cobb, "That Orchard is the most extraordinary man, just like somebody in a store."

He asked me if I would like to meet him and I said I would. So he took me out to the penitentiary and told the warden that I would like to see Orchard.

The warden said, "Mercy, why?"

"I don't know," Mr. Cobb said, "just let him come in a minute."

So he came in. He was very polite and quiet. He said, "I've heard a lot about you, Miss Barrymore."

"I've heard a certain amount about you," I said.

That was all—one of the shortest conversations on record.

That night the lovely old Boise theater was jammed. Every newspaperman of any importance from all over the world was covering the trial and they were all in the theater. It was a thrilling audience to play to.

When I went to the train after the theater, a little Pinkerton man, who had been working under cover on the railroads to get evidence, brought me a bunch of flowers. The whole day was a fabulous experience.

On that tour when we played a one-night stand in Lincoln, Nebraska, I decided that since I had so much time to spare during the day and couldn't carry a piano about with me, I ought to learn to play the violin. So I went to a music store and bought one. I had my first lesson from an old German professor in Lincoln who was very kind but rather bewildered by my wanting to play the violin. I carried mine around with me for a long time but I was never very good at it.

When we were in New Orleans I gave a lovely Christmas party at Antoine's for the whole company. We had a big, bright room with all the famous Antoine specialties. I remember their turning out the lights when they brought in the great trays of flaming *oranges brûlées*. The Kearneys were there and Cousin Georgie and Bee and Mrs. Pitt, Arthur Bryson, Lumsden Hare and Charlie Hammond, whom I always called the only Tasmanian in captivity. He actually did come from Tasmania.

I remember that it was the time of hobble skirts, but the fashion hadn't reached the South when we got there and when my cousin Bee wore her hobble in the streets, taking tiny steps, crowds of people used to follow her. Bee, who was always very unaware of people around her, paid no attention to them. She just said, "That is what they're wearing."

It was on that tour that a colored maid in a southern hotel was very anxious to do something for me, and when I couldn't think of anything that needed doing, she said sorrowfully, "You never have nothing did, does you?"

Charlie and Lumsden Hare used to play golf together. One night, after playing at a country club and dining very well, they were late in getting to the theater and everybody else was practically on the stage. Lumsden was supposed to play the part of a hearty Englishman, the uncle of the man I was going to marry, and when he came on in the first act, he was supposed to say, "You mustn't mind me, my dear, I'm just a bit of the roast beef of old England."

But that night he said, "You mustn't mind me, my dear, I'm just a piece of old roast beef."

Nobody could speak, but James Kearney knew enough to ring down the curtain. Luckily the act was almost over so it didn't make much difference.

We played well into the summer in *Captain Jinks*. My brother Lionel and his wife were living in Paris and that summer I went over to see them. We had a delightful apartment in the Avenue Marceau. During that summer I went on a motor trip with Millie Sutherland through France. We went from Paris to Normandy, and stopped at that beautiful, famous inn, Guillaume le Conquérant. We used to motor over to play golf at Deauville from there, and we would go to shop and see the sights at Trouville. Sometimes we went to the theater in the evening or watched the gambling.

I left Millie at the Guillaume le Conquérant and went to England to sail from there, and to see the play I was to do the next season, called *Lady Frederick*, by W. Somerset Maugham.

The theaters in London seemed more wonderful than ever. There was always something special for me about going to the theater there; I could go to see the same play again and again, and like it just as much the last time as the first. I saw *The Merry Widow* fourteen times, with Joe Coyne and Lillie Elsie, the best cast and the most beautiful production in the world. In other years I saw Beerbohm Tree's production of *Julius Caesar* twelve times and *The Gay Lord Quex* almost as many. I shall never forget the marvelous revues at the Gaiety and Gertie Millar, and I shall always vividly remember Dan Leno, a truly great artist in the music halls, who not only made you laugh but broke your heart.

In September I was back in New York to begin rehearsing in *Lady Frederick*. Before going down to spend the weekend with Uncle Jack at East Hampton, I was having lunch at Sherry's with him, Aunt Dodo and Bee and two or three other people who were also coming down for the weekend. A young man strolled by the table and Uncle Jack said, "Hello, Hungry. Sit down."

So Russell Colt sat down. He was spending the weekend at East Hampton, too, and rode down on the train with us. After we got there he drifted away, but he came back to Uncle Jack's after dinner and after that, well, it just happened. That's all. Quickly. Very quickly. It didn't take long for me to discover that this was it and that this time there was no escape.

I don't remember that during the six months of our engagement I even tried to escape. Russell had tremendous humor and at first his lighthearted irresponsibility—he never really grew up—seemed only to add to his tremendous charm. It was a happy time for me, untroubled by any doubts.

Colonel Colt, Russell's father, however, was not quite so untroubled. This was just after what was artlessly considered in those days to be a panic, and like many other men who had been very rich, Colonel Colt was for the time being feeling very poor. He asked me to come and see him at the old Holland House where he was living in one room, and when I met him there, in the huge parlor, two stories high and a thousand miles long, he said, "I can't understand why you want to marry my son. I have no money."

I said, "I don't want money."

He said, "How are you going to live?"

I said, "I make enough money, but I think it would be a good thing if Russell had some kind of job."

And Colonel Colt arranged with H. L. Horton and Co., a Wall Street firm in which he had an interest, that after we were married Russell was to be a junior partner.

We decided to be married when *Lady Frederick* was playing in Boston, and I went to see Bishop O'Connell to arrange for a dispensation to marry a Protestant. The Bishop —who was later to be Cardinal—completely fascinated Russell when Russell went to see him to sign the necessary papers. When he came away, Russell said, "That's the most charming man I ever met. How do you get to be a Catholic?"

But he never did anything about it.

I had red dispatch boxes filled with letters from everybody I had ever known. I tore them all up. It seemed to be the thing to do, to make a clean break. I felt that all my energies must be devoted now to my new life which was going to be my married life, and to my work in the theater. I had those two things to do and they seemed to be enough.

XV

Oh, Let's See Her Die!

After the play on Saturday I went to stay with the Fairchilds in Dedham. The Episcopal minister there, a friend of theirs, made all the arrangements with the priest at Hyde Park to marry us. The ceremony took place on Sunday morning between masses in the priest's house at the Church of the Most Precious Blood. Jack Barrymore and Russell's brother, Roswell Colt, were the only witnesses. It was a short ceremony, lasting just a few minutes. Russell was curious and interested because so much of it was in Latin. We went back to Dedham, and the next day I went back to the play.

I didn't want anything in the newspapers before the marriage, and the news of it didn't leak out until several days afterward when I didn't mind it.

Our honeymoon was the rest of the tour in *Lady Frederick*, which took us all the way to California. When we played in San Francisco, Russell and I went down to spend a week-end with Sam Morse and his wife, Anne, at Merced, where Sam had been given his first job, in charge of Mr. Crocker's huge ranch. Anne was expecting her Sammy then, as I was expecting mine, and she and I sat on the porch and rocked while Sam and Russell went out shooting ducks.

I hadn't yet been to see a doctor because I knew if I went to one he might tell me that I couldn't finish the season, and I knew I had to do that.

Uncle Jack was also closing his season in California, and I arranged things so that we could come back on the same train with him and Aunt Dodo. I was getting, not frightened exactly, but a little nervous, as there had been no one for me to talk to about having a baby, and Aunt Dodo was the nearest thing to a family that I had. She was the one who got me the wonderful nurse, Mrs. Frings, who took care of me.

When I came back to New York, I went to see the only doctor I knew, Dr. Bagg, who had been Mummum's doctor. His brownstone house in the Fifties was boarded up, as most of those houses used to be every summer, with a sign saying "Back in September."

I didn't know what to do, but one night in Greenwich, where we took a house for the summer, I met two awfully nice women—Margery Close and Maribell Coffin. Russell had gone to New Haven with Maribell's husband. After dinner the two girls asked me what doctor I had and when I said the only one I knew would not be back until September, they told me about theirs and that was how I came to know my dear Dr. Danforth, a wonderful man. He had discreet little side whiskers that inspired Uncle Jack to call him "storm at sea."

He and Mrs. Danforth were spending the summer in Greenwich, and he was reassuring and kind and made me feel safe—a very wonderful feeling.

After Russell had been commuting from Mamaroneck to New York for some little time, Temple Gwathney, a Greenwich friend of his, asked him what train he took and Russell said, "I usually miss the 10:37."

At that time there was another young man in the employ of Horton and Company who took his work and his life a little more seriously. His name was Frank McIntyre. Mr.

O'Keefe, one of the partners, took an interest in him, and when he found out that young McIntyre had a vocation for the priesthood, he helped him through a theological seminary, where he must have continued to be serious about his work and his life. He is now James Francis Cardinal McIntyre of Los Angeles.

Lionel and Doris came back from Paris that summer and stayed with us at Greenwich for a while. It was great to be with Lionel, one of the very few times that it happened after we were small children. He seemed to know about everything in the world, just like Uncle Jack.

In the fall we moved into New York where we took the August Belmont, Jr., house on Thirty-fourth Street. One Sunday morning Russell and I had arranged to go to Garden City to spend the day with Peter and Margaret Dunne. Russell was going to play golf with Benjie Guinness and Peter, and I was to sit on the porch and rock with Margaret Dunne till the men came back to lunch.

But just before I got up to dress, the nurse Aunt Dodo had found for me stopped in on her way to visit her mother in Canada. She asked me what I was going to do that morning, and I said I was going down to Garden City.

"How do you feel?" she asked.

I said, "I feel all right now, but in the night I had a sort of pain and took some Jamaica ginger."

"Jamaica ginger?" she said. "I don't think you'd better go. I am going to call Dr. Danforth."

She did and he came down.

He said, "You're not going to Garden City today. You're going to have your baby today."

I said, "I can't. I can't have him till January."

But Sammy was born that night, November 28, an eight-months baby. He weighed only three and a half pounds. Doctors take seven-months babies in their stride, but for some reason eight-months babies are alarming.

Dr. Danforth didn't believe in incubators so we had an electric pad under the mattress of Sammy's crib. Mrs. Frings, the nurse, did not go to Canada. She stayed with me for a year and it was probably she more than anybody else who saved Sammy's life. From the moment of his arrival, she took me and the household in hand and managed us with a rod of iron.

It was her idea that a photograph should be taken of the baby and me immediately, so a photographer was summoned and I was propped up in bed with pillows, a lace cap put on my head and, I suppose, registered maternity under the stern orders of Mrs. Frings, my nurse, and the small son was placed in my arms. That picture went all over the world; I received copies of it from China, Japan and India.

My father-in-law asked if I would name the baby after his Uncle Samuel, the inventor of the Colt revolver, because nobody had yet been named after him. (Colonel Colt was named Samuel Pomeroy Colt, but he was always called Pomeroy.) I said I would be delighted, and two months later there was a wonderful baptism in the cathedral. The two godfathers were Peter Dunne and Jack Barrymore and when during the ceremony the priest told them to say the Apostles' Creed, Jack began confidently, "I believe in

God, the Father Almighty, Creator of heaven and earth," and then he said, "That lets me out."

Peter Dunne knew it all of course. He had three brothers who were priests. His face got purple trying not to laugh at Jack.

They all came back to the house, where I left them celebrating and went to play in *Mid-Channel,* in which I had been rehearsing three weeks after Sammy's birth.

Mid-Channel, a problem play by Arthur Pinero, was a distinct departure from the plays I had been doing. It has always been one of my favorites.

I had a telephone put into my dressing room at the Empire Theatre because I was always wanting to call up and find out about Sammy, and of course I wanted his nurse to be able to reach me. It was the first time, to my knowledge, that a telephone had been put into a dressing room, and certainly the first time for such a reason.

We went on living in the Belmont house, but I told Colonel Colt that I thought it would be good for everybody if we could live in the country. Colonel Colt had recovered quickly from the idea that he was bankrupt. He said, "You find a place and I'll give it to you."

So, all that summer, after I finished my tour in *Mid-Channel,* we looked at houses on Long Island, in Westchester, everywhere, and at last we found the house in Mamaroneck that is still ours. I remember the first time I went into it I said, "What a lovely hall for a little boy to throw his cap in."

Russell didn't like it. He thought I was crazy to want it, and there was plenty of reason for him to think so. The

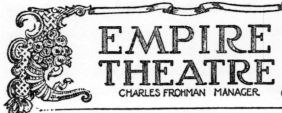

EMPIRE THEATRE

CHARLES FROHMAN MANAGER

Evenings 8.15.   Matinees Wednesday and Saturday 2.15.

CHARLES FROHMAN
Presents

Ethel Barrymore
IN A PLAY IN FOUR ACTS.
Mid=Channel
BY
SIR ARTHUR W. PINERO

THEODORE BLUNDELL..............................CHARLES DALTON
THE HON. PETER MOTTRAM.......................H. REEVES SMITH
LEONARD FERRIS..ERIC MATURIN
WARREN, servant at Lancaster Gate....................CHARLES WRIGHT
COLE, servant at the flat in Cavendish Square................EDWIN ARNOLD
RIDEOUT, Mr. Ferris's servant..................A. ROMAINE CALLENDER
UPHOLSTERERS....................................... { T. RUSSELL
                                                   { ...J. KELLY
ZOE BLUNDELL..............................ETHEL BARRYMORE
MRS. PIERPONT................................PHOEBE COYNE
ETHEL PIERPONT..............................LOUISE RUTTER
MRS. ANNERLY................................NINA SEVENING
LENA...MARIANNE THURBER

PROGRAM CONTINUED ON SECOND PAGE FOLLOWING.

"Special Notice" on this program, March, 1910, will interest present-day theater goers.

house was painted red—barn red—with black shutters, and Russell couldn't see it, as I did, white, with green shutters. It was dark inside, too, and although all the other fireplaces—and there was one in every room, even on the third floor—had white marble mantelpieces, beautifully plain, the mantelpiece in the library was a horror of wooden curlicues, with green silk backing them. I drew a perfectly plain Adamsy one, and a local carpenter, Mr. Morton, made it, and it made—and still makes—the room.

After Colonel Colt went to look the place over he said I could have a desk in a real-estate office if I wanted one because I had picked out a really marvelous piece of property.

The place is on Taylor's Lane, which was named after old Mr. Taylor, who built the big house for himself and the other houses along the lane for his children. It is twenty-one miles away from New York and might just as well be a million miles away from it. There are nine or ten acres of land, and the young apple trees in the orchard that I planted are great trees now. My daughter Ethel and my son Jackie were born there, and Ethel lives there now. My chauffeur, David Britt, who came to me when he was nineteen and has been with me for forty years, looks after the place. Carved on a cornerstone of an old building in the village is the inscription "Britt 1682." That was when his family came from England to Mamaroneck. Britt has four grandchildren now. He has been of inestimable service to me and I am ever grateful for his faithfulness.

In January I played a short engagement in *Trelawny of the Wells* and followed it with Barrie's one-act play, *The*

Twelve Pound Look, preceded by a revival of *Alice-Sit-by-the Fire.*

Although I loved *The Twelve Pound Look* and it was a great success, I had no idea that it was to serve as a lifesaver for the next twenty-five years.

Jack was with me in *Alice-Sit-by-the-Fire.* He had recently married Katherine Corri Harris, a lovely young girl, who was always my favorite sister-in-law. She had just come home from France, where she had been in school, and at the first dance she went to she met Jack, and that was the end of her as Katherine Harris. I was at their wedding in the Church of St. Francis Xavier, and I remember how beautifully radiant they both looked with the sun shining on them through a stained-glass window. They came to live with us for a while at Mamaroneck and then took an apartment in Gramercy Square.

We spent that summer at Mamaroneck, a marvelous summer for me with my year-and-a-half-old son.

Colonel Colt made us an unbirthday present of a De Dion-Bouton car, with a hood that stretched out half a block in front of me as Britt taught me to drive on the country roads. It was a terrific car, but I was always panicky for fear children would run out in front of it.

In the fall I began rehearsing in *The Witness for the Defense* in which, before opening in New York, I went on tour. Mr. Frohman arranged this so that I might open in New York in the Empire, in which invariably Uncle Jack opened on Labor Day, to be followed after eight or ten weeks by Maude Adams, and she in turn to be followed by me, as the third of Mr. Frohman's stars.

When we went on tour Sister was on the way and in South Bend I very nearly lost her. The doctor whom the hotel called for me was astonished to find that I wanted to keep my child. He seemed to think that, because I was an actress, I wouldn't want to. I was almost angry enough to kill him, but I didn't lose my temper or my baby. I came back to New York and opened at the Empire in *The Witness for the Defense* and then played in a revival of *Cousin Kate,* preceded by *A Slice of Life,* by Barrie.

This was a sort of burlesque of domestic drama and Jack came back to me for this play. It was funny, and the audience loved it. We played it for four weeks at the Empire Theatre. At the end of March we stopped and I went to Mamaroneck to wait for Sister.

I was at the stage of just sitting on the porch, not moving around much, when suddenly our English butler, a very good one, came out of the dining room, stood in front of me and fixed his eye on me. I thought he was going to tell me that dinner was served but instead he said, "Madame, do you know Lillian Russell?"

I said, "Yes, I do."

He said, "She must be a very beautiful woman."

I was frightened to death of him. I saw that he was staring at me, not really seeing me, I thought.

"Yes," I said. "She is, and I think I'll go in now."

We had to let him go. Afterward we had a man who had been Winston Churchill's butler. I remember seeing him when Winston had a small house in Half Moon Street and I dined there. But one night when dinner seemed to be awfully late, I opened the dining-room door and found that nothing had been started. Russell went up to the man's room and found him lying on his bed fully dressed and fully drunk with *Tattlers* and *Sketches* scattered all over him.

That was the end of male servants in the house.

Sister was born on April 30, much to the indignation of Mary, my dresser, who wanted her to be a May baby.

It was Dr. Danforth who named Sister. I was still unconscious when the reporters called, and the doctor answered the telephone. He said, "It's a little girl."

They said, "What are they going to name her?"

And he said, "Ethel, of course."

I was horrified when I heard about it, but I couldn't bear to hurt Dr. Danforth's feelings.

I didn't like any of the plays that Mr. Frohman gave me to read that summer and at last I went to him and suggested that I play *The Twelve Pound Look* in vaudeville. He threw up his hands in horror.

I said, "Why not? Irene Vanbrugh, who originally played the part in London, is playing it in the halls there. Bernhardt has played in vaudeville. Why all this snobbishness, or whatever it is, about it?"

He had no suitable play for me and I, as usual, had no suitable income so he finally agreed to let me play it on the Orpheum Circuit because that was out West. He sent for Charlie Dillingham and said, "Ethel thinks she wants to play *The Twelve Pound Look* in vaudeville. Take her to see Martin Beck."

So Charlie Dillingham took me to see Martin Beck, who wrote something on a little piece of paper and handed it to me. He said, "Would this be all right?"

I said, "Fine."

The paper read $3,000 a week. It was a very exciting envelope to open every Saturday. I wonder where it has all gone.

I played the Orpheum Circuit all over the West. Then I wrote to Mr. Frohman and asked why I couldn't play all over the East and I did for a whole year. In *The Twelve Pound Look* I twice broke the Palace Theatre record. Monday-afternoon openings at the Palace were really spectacular. Dana Gibson was only one of the many, many famous people who never failed to be there.

It was demanding—but very rewarding. I learned so much watching the other artists. I found out that you have to be awfully good in vaudeville. It is a real taskmaster because there are so many acts in it, like slack-wire artists, for instance, that require absolute perfection.

The vaudeville theaters all over the country proved to be beautiful, not only in the front of the house, but in the back as well. The performers seemed to have been remembered by the architect; the dressing rooms were nearly always superior to those in any other class of theaters. Things ran as systematically and efficiently as in a large business concern. I loved everybody I met—all the people on the bill with me—and I was never tired of standing in the wings watching the different "turns."

The vaudeville public is an exacting one and nothing must ever be slurred for them—perfect in the afternoon and perfect at night, over and over again for weeks and weeks.

For instance, a slack-wire artist who does somersaults, swaying out over the audience, has to land on the wire or he's dead. The audience takes his perfection for granted, and if you follow him, you've got to be as good in your job as he is in his, or you might as well be dead. The audience are so used to perfection that they are tough.

Once when Lionel was playing in vaudeville, he was standing in the wings to watch Bert Williams' technique, as he did at every performance. One of the stagehands said, "Like him, huh?"

Lionel said, "Yes. He's terrific."

And the stagehand said, just as Williams came off stage and passed him, "Yeah, he's a good nigger, knows his place."

And Williams mumbled, "Yes. A good nigger. Knows his place. Going there now. Dressing room ONE!"

After those two years any time I didn't have a play that I could bear to do I went back to vaudeville with *The Twelve Pound Look,* and every time I went it was good for me. Those exacting audiences loved the play, and I played it for years and years.

When I was playing *The Twelve Pound Look* at Keith's in Washington, I came back to the hotel at ten o'clock and found that the door of my sitting room was unlocked. Just as I opened it, I heard a cry from Mary, my dresser, who had gone in through the bedroom door. My big trunk was open and its contents scattered all over the room. On the floor, empty, was the box in which I had kept my jewelry—two rings of my mother's, the only things I had of hers, and the lovely diamond watch, pearl bracelet, and big diamond pin and other things that Colonel Colt had given me. The robbery must have been done by someone who had a key to the room and knew that I kept the jewelry box in the bottom of my trunk.

The hotel people were awfully rude, practically suggesting that it was just one of those publicity schemes, and I was very angry with them. I called up Nick Longworth, who was then Representative from Ohio, and, as soon as he came over, the hotel people were apologetic, and I disliked them more than ever.

The jewels were never recovered. They were about the only ones I ever had and I was very depressed about losing them.

Colonel Colt was always very generous and kind to me and to the children. When Sammy was a year old, the Colonel gave him a toy fort with soldiers from every regiment in the world in it, and of course all that Sammy could do with it at that age was to kick it to pieces. Later the Colonel gave him a cart with two live goats to pull it, so well trained that Sammy could drive it himself with a nurse hovering nearby.

Ida, my Swedish nurse, came to us when Sister was about a year old. She was a superb baby nurse, *the* baby nurse of New York. She paid very little attention to Sammy, but she adored Sister until Jackie was born, when Sister ceased to exist for her.

When Sister was about two, she was being treated for what was thought to be croup, but Ida didn't like the sound of her breathing and I didn't either. So I tried to get Dr. Emmett Holt, the great baby specialist. He couldn't come but promised to send his assistant, Dr. Bartlett, who, he said, was better than he was. So Dr. Bartlett came out to Mamaroneck and in a matter of seconds he had diagnosed the case as diphtheria, the baby was wrapped up, and we were on our way in the car to Minton Hospital, the only place in New York that would take contagious diseases. It was a private wing of the Willard Parker Hospital, and thank God Dr. Bartlett knew about it.

I stayed in the room next to Sister's. Both of us were getting many units of antitoxin. It was a miracle that Sister didn't die. Once when I was standing beside her bed with Dr. Bartlett and Dr. Danforth, I saw them look at each other and thought they were going to tell me that this was it. Suddenly Sister opened her eyes, looked up and said, "Hello, Mummie." And there was the miracle.

That was in July and in September Jackie was born. I remember calling Mr. Frohman on the telephone about two hours afterward and telling him that I would be ready for rehearsals very soon and that I had an awfully nice little boy. I shall never forget the sound that came from the other end of the telephone. He could hardly believe his ears.

He exclaimed, "It is impossible for you to be talking!"

"No," I said, "I am quite all right and will be ready soon." That was all I was allowed to say to him but I remember it gave me great amusement to do it.

So ten days after Jackie came into the world, I was on the Empire stage rehearsing in *Tante,* a play Haddon Chambers had written from the book by Anne Sedgwick, with a most interesting part for me.

The furnished house in Sixty-first Street that I had rented for three years so as to have the children with me when I was playing in New York was no longer big enough. It had been all right for two children, but there wasn't room enough in it for three, and I took rooms for Sammy and his mademoiselle in the Netherlands, just around the corner, near enough to let me have all three children with me almost as much as if we all had been under one roof.

I always spent every possible minute with them, but I also always had the most perfectly competent nurses, because I never did presume to know all about children and I wanted everything to be right for mine. They were simply heaven, the most important thing in my life. They are the reason why I know it was written that I was to marry Russell Colt and nobody else. If anybody else had been their father, they wouldn't have been the same children; they couldn't possibly have been nicer children, or as nice.

They were so completely different from each other I always felt, as they grew up, that I might have picked them up from different orphan asylums—but believe me I didn't!

More and more as things began to go wrong, or not so well, with my marriage, they were my happiness. And more and more, as things kept on going not so well, there was blessed sanctuary, every night, in those two and a half hours in the theater.

When people ask me if it is possible to combine marriage with a career I have always replied, "I was born and so, I've always understood, was my mother." We all had careers and marriage and children. My own career, instead of interfering with my marriage, helped to make it possible and helped me to keep on trying, as long and determinedly as I did, to save it.

I had waited so long to be sure it was the right one that I couldn't let it fail. I wanted desperately to save it, and for a long time, largely because of that career of mine, I did save it.

There are plenty of happy memories of those years to set

off against the unhappy ones. The memory, for instance, of winter nights when the children slept on the open sleeping porch at Mamaroneck, and I would come home from the theater and go out to see them, and their cheeks would be like red apples from the cold, but when I put my hand down under the covers they were warm as toast.

. . . And the memory of the time I read Sammy the Mother Goose rhyme:

> Little Miss Muffet sat on a tuffet
> Eating of curds and whey;
> There came a great spider and sat down beside her
> And frightened Miss Muffet away.

and Sammy, thinking for a minute, and then saying: "Where was her mother?"—an observation that to my knowledge no other child ever made.

. . . And the memory of the time I took him to see *Peter Pan* and he was so depressed, after the children had flown, that I asked him what was the matter and he said:

"Where do that mother and father think those children are?"

. . . And I remember the sign at the end of our lane that said, TAYLOR'S LANE. GO SLOW. And Ida, the big Swedish nurse, always reading it aloud as she drove by, and Sammy and Sister saying it with her—and the great day when we were driving past it and Jackie, who so far in his two years of life had alarmingly never uttered, suddenly said, with a strong Swedish accent: "Taylor's Lane. Go slow."

And how delighted we all were and how we laughed!

. . . And the club at Manursing Island and Sister as a little

Russell G. Colt (Culver Service)

Miss Barrymore with her three children (left
to right), Ethel Barrymore Colt, John Drew
Colt and Samuel Colt (Spencer Berger Collection)

Ethel Barrymore with her first child,
Samuel Colt (Culver Service)

The Colt children riding in
Central Park

Miss Barrymore and her
children meet in Hollywood
(Culver Service)

Early photographs of John Barrymore (left) and Lionel Barrymore (Spencer Berger Collection)

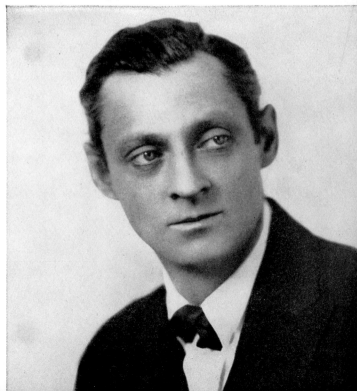

The Empire Theatre during the run of *Clair de Lune* (Culver Service)

Unfurling the Equity strike flag
(Culver Service)

Ethel Barrymore supporting the Actors'
Strike in 1919 (Culver Service)

Miss Barrymore in *Clair de Lune* (Culver Service)

With Louis Calhern in *The Love Duel*, 1929 (Spencer Berger Collection)

As the 101-year-old grandmother in *Whiteoaks* (Spencer Berger Collection)

As Portia in *The Merchant of Venice*, with Walter Hampden (Courtesy, Museum of the City of New York)

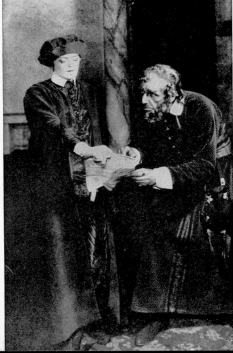

In *The Second Mrs. Tanqueray* (Culver Service)

The Lady of the Camellias (Culver Service)

Miss Barrymore in *Rose Bernd*
(Culver Service)

With Eva Le Gallienne in *L'Aiglon* (Culver Service)

girl winning all the cups for diving—and winning them again as a young lady.

. . . And the time I called for my children at a party given by Dorothy Caruso for her brother's children and some of their little friends. I was early, and the children were still sitting around the table with their paper caps on, eating ice cream. Dorothy murmured, "Go in the next room. Enrico is in there."

So I went in. Caruso was walking up and down with the baby, Gloria, in his arms, humming her to sleep. It was a high moment.

. . . And the time I yielded to Sammy's and Sister's beseechings and had Britt drive us to Coney Island. And what a long walk it was to Luna Park from where we left the car, with Ida carrying Jackie and me leading Sammy and Sister by the hand. And how every few steps we'd pass a hot dog stand. I had known that we would and that as always the smell of hot dogs would make me deathly sick, but I felt I must do my duty by my children and had brought along three handkerchiefs saturated with Atkinson's White Rose and breathed through them. (Atkinson's White Rose was the only perfume I ever loved. I used to get it from London but during the Second World War they stopped making it and afterward they were never able to get one of the vital ingredients.) I let the children ride on the merry-go-round but not on the roller coaster. At Rye there was a park with a roller coaster and I made Sammy and Jackie promise never to ride on it, but of course they did.

. . . And the Fourth of July visits to Colonel Colt's house at Bristol, Rhode Island—going up on the Fall River boat

with the three children and two nurses and being met
by two Rolls Royces and by Wheeler, Colonel Colt's very
English butler, who would be standing at the very edge of
the dock, swaying slightly, so that I was always alarmed lest
he sway too far and fall between the boat and the dock. But
though he always swayed, he never swayed too far and
always maintained his impeccable dignity.

(Years later I went to dinner in Boston with Governor and
Mrs. Fuller. One reason I was asked was that Augustus John
was staying with them. He had stayed with them all summer in New Hampshire, painting the family, and he was
finishing them up in Boston. I knew it was a teetotal house
and I wondered how Augustus John, a convivial soul, was
taking it. And when I rang the bell who do you think opened
the door of the magnificent house on Beacon Street?
Wheeler, still swaying. I knew then that Augustus John
would be all right and he was. I sat next to him at dinner
and he was feeling no pain whatever.)

Colonel Colt's house was lovely, with a wonderfully beautiful staircase. It was built by one of Russell's De Wolfe
ancestors. There were always a host of De Wolfes at those
Fourth of July celebrations and hosts of Colts and Senator
Green who is still flourishing and all the Herreshoffs, the
yacht builders, whose boats, especially those designed by
the blind one, were never beaten. The children loved the
parade, in which Colonel Colt drove in the big family coach,
which was always brought out for the day, almost as impos-
ing as the royal coach except for not being gilded. The
children loved the great Colt farm, too, fifteen miles of it
on Narragansett Bay, with great Percheron horses and beautiful Jersey cows and, of course, endless litters of pigs. Once

when we were coming back from the farm when Sammy was about six he said, "I saw the loveliest little pink pigs—but," with a Gallic gesture of fastidious disgust, reminiscent of his mademoiselle, "oh, the mother!"

Those were good years, when the children were little and I could have them with me nearly all the time. Russell had discovered bronchitis and decided that it was necessary for him to spend the winters at Palm Beach where, luckily, Horton and Company had an office, but he was at Mamaroneck much of the rest of the time, and I still hoped—and sometimes I believed—that I could save my marriage.

We had a strong bond in our common love of sports. We went to many baseball games together. I remember going to Philadelphia and Pittsburgh to see the World Series. And I love to remember the time when we took the Sutherlands and their daughter Rosemary and Eric Chaplin and Philip Sassoon to a game between the Yankees and Detroit at old Yankee field. The crowd was very much interested in our party but didn't know who my friends were. Millie looked like somebody important, and the photographers came and stood in front of our box, which our English guests didn't even notice. The Yankees and Detroit were supposed to be the two best teams in the American League that year, and they had great players like Ty Cobb. The stadium was packed, but for some reason it was a day of disaster for the outfielders. They made many errors and suddenly Rosemary, a lovely-looking child, with a high English voice, turned around and said, "Jolly bad fielders, aren't they?"

The whole crowd roared, and they gave her a standing ovation—of which she also was unaware.

We often went together to polo games at Westbury. I had

been passionately devoted to polo ever since Maude Waterbury and I had sat on top of a four-in-hand coach at Hurlingham to watch Larry and Monty and Foxhall Keene play the English team in the first international matches ever held and, to the astonishment of the English (to say nothing of their own), to win. I remember that Larry was wearing spurs that drew blood on his gray pony and Lord Shrewsbury, the referee, made him take them off.

We saw some wonderful polo at Westbury and some wonderful tennis at Forest Hills and some wonderful fights at Madison Square Garden during those years.

They seem, even now, to have been good years.

I have often been asked why I didn't like football. I said I didn't know football because all my life I had a matinee on Saturday. Once we did go to the Polo Grounds on a very cold Sunday afternoon to see one of the very first professional football games. And I remember Russell's saying that professional football would never last.

Often we went to see the Castles dancing—how thrilling it was—or to see Maurice and Florence Walton. We took the Medill McCormicks there, I remember.

Russell and I used to go to Judge Gary's to play poker. Millionaires like the Spreckels played in the big game somewhere high upstairs. We played in a milder one on the second floor. Judge Gary himself never played and neither did Charlie Whitman, who was often there, just looking on.

We also saw Charlie Whitman in court when we went one day to the Becker trial. I don't know why we went, but we did and I still vividly remember Becker—I sat much too close to him—and Judge Seabury on the bench and the deadly seriousness of the whole procedure. The case really grew out of a brilliant job of reporting by a young man on the New York *World*, the same Herbert Bayard Swope with whom Jack had once shared rooms. He was on the scene of the murder soon after it happened and got word of it to Charlie Whitman who was in Newport. If Mr. Whitman had not returned to New York so quickly, he probably would not have found the evidence on which Becker and the gunmen were convicted.

The case fascinated the foreign press, and I remember the beautifully Gallic translations that the French newspapers made the names of the gunmen, Gyp le Sanguinaire for Gyp the Blood, Louis le Gauche for Lefty Louis and Louis le Blanc for Whitey Lewis.

Several times we went to Saratoga in August for the races, first with two children and then with three. We would have one of the little cottages that belonged to the United States Hotel, an extraordinary place with huge chandeliers and a terrific lot of character and atmosphere that seemed to belong back in the 1800's. It always fascinated me, and so did Canfield's, where everybody dined.

At the end of the season of the *Tante* year I played in a revival of *A Scrap of Paper* with Uncle Jack at the Empire Theatre. It was charming to be playing with my uncle again after so long—and not carrying a tray. This is a good place, perhaps, for me to stop and talk about him.

Although I had seen him at Mummum's house and at North Long Branch in summer when I was very young, my first real memories of Uncle Jack begin when I came back from Canada and went to live with Mummum, who was

EMPIRE THEATRE

CHARLES FROHMAN MANAGER

Evenings at 8.30.   Matinees Wednesdays and Saturdays at 2.20.

FOR A LIMITED NUMBER OF PERFORMANCES.

CHARLES FROHMAN

PRESENTS

JOHN   ETHEL
DREW BARRYMORE

IN A COMEDY IN THREE ACTS, ENTITLED

A SCRAP OF PAPER

By VICTORIEN SARDOU.

CAST OF CHARACTERS.

PROSPER COURAMONT ....JOHN DREW
BARON DE LA GLACIERE...........................CHARLES DALTON
BRISEMOUCHE, *Naturalist*............................ FULLER MELLISH
ANATOLE, *his ward*............................ERNEST GLENDINNING
BAPTISTE ....WALTER SODERLING
FRANCOIS .... FRANK McCOY
   SUZANNE DE RUSEVILLE....................ETHEL BARRYMORE
   LOUISE DE LA GLACIERE.........................MARY BOLAND
   MATHILDE .... CHARLOTTE IVES
   MLLE. ZENOBIE.................................JEFFREYS LEWIS
   MADAME DUPONT...................MRS. THOMAS WHIFFEN
   PAULINE .... HELEN COLLIER

PROGRAM CONTINUED ON SECOND PAGE FOLLOWING.

staying in his apartment at the Sherman Square Hotel. But I didn't see very much of him there; he was either rehearsing or playing, and I was looking for a job. I took his charm, his urbanity, his sophistication as matters of course: he was Mummum's son, my mother's brother; what could he be but perfect? (I wasn't in awe of him, though. I was never in awe of anyone except Mummum, and that was devotion, rather than awe, the feeling that I couldn't have borne to disappoint her in any way.)

I didn't really begin to know Uncle Jack until I went on tour with him, but I already had some realization of his amazing omniscience. As children we were always trying to stump him with a question he couldn't answer. Once we found a word in the encyclopedia that we were sure he wouldn't know, but when we asked him, he said, without looking up from his book, "A small Persian prayer rug."

That was characteristic of him; everything he did, in life or on the stage, seemed effortless, and his profound knowledge seemed effortless, too.

John Drew's acting was so perfectly effortless that it didn't seem to be acting. Some people used to say, without realizing what a tribute they were paying him, that he only played himself, that "he didn't act but just behaved."

The perfection of his acting made it possible and easy for him to play jokes while he was on the stage without the audience suspecting that he was doing it.

He had a little humorous demon that always prompted him to try to "break up" the other person on the stage with him. I remember his doing it to me in *Rosemary*. When we had spent the summer at North Long Branch the train had stopped at a little station called Low Moor, and when I was on the stage with him in *Rosemary* he would keep saying, under his breath, as I talked: "The next station will be Low Moor. The next station will be Low Moor," which of course meant that he was amused by my voice, rising out of the depths.

He finally managed to make me giggle and a newspaper critic said I wasn't taking my work seriously.

While I was on tour with him, he and Arthur Byron often used to do such things to each other. One night on a one-night stand Uncle Jack's valet, Albert, whom we always called Albert the Good, produced a dress shirt that had come back from the laundry shiny-bright as a mirror. Uncle Jack made a terrible row about it, but it was the only one there was, and he had to wear it. Arthur Byron, as soon as they were on the stage, pretended to use the shirt as a mirror, twirling his mustache in front of it, and adjusting his tie. And once when Arthur had on a shiny shirt, Uncle Jack did the same thing to him. They were so skillful that they could do such things to each other without the audience knowing what was going on. The only person from whom he never elicited even a smile was Maude Adams.

One of my years with him was in a play called *That Imprudent Young Couple* about two Englishmen in a Middle East country, in which Arthur was the villain. At the end of one scene Uncle Jack was supposed to say to Arthur, "You say there are 12,982 pounds in the coffers. All I can find is 6,000."

One night he said, instead, "You say there are 6,892 pounds in the coffers. All I can find is 12,000." He said it with great authority and sternness. And there was absolutely nothing for Arthur to say in answer, and the curtain had to come down.

"Break up" stories aren't nearly as funny to anybody else as they are for actors on the stage. They must touch some special nervous chord that only actors know about. These jokes of Uncle Jack's seemed very, very funny to me then and they seem just as funny to me now.

Uncle Jack was the author of many of the words and phrases that became part of our family vocabulary. One of them, that always amused us when we were young was his calling Henry Quatre, "The Angry Cat." Another was his nicknaming Lionel "The Bible-backed Beethoven," when Lionel used to sit for hours at the piano at East Hampton playing jazz.

Uncle Jack's clothes always seemed so absolutely right. Whenever he got off the train in London, he would say, "Poole and Peal, I'm with you again."

As children and afterward we were always thrilled by his Charvet shirts and ties and pajamas and dressing gowns—in which Lionel and Jack, after visits to East Hampton, would often appear.

Uncle Jack's house was in East Hampton—one of the most beautiful villages in America, with magnificent old trees and a village green the like of which isn't to be found anywhere else. Uncle Jack was greatly beloved there—they called him "The Squire." Everybody was always so delighted to see him when he went, every morning, to the post office, sometimes riding, sometimes driving a horse and cart, later driving a car. He loved to ride. There were stables and a big paddock behind his house.

Almost from the beginning of his long career he stood at

the very top of his profession, as high in the affectionate regard of his fellow actors as in that of the people who knew him only as a person—the person—of the play. To all of these, all over the country, in large cities and little ones, his coming was always an event and his name on the billboards was of itself enough to make a success of any play.

He was always wonderfully considerate of others. When I played with him in *A Scrap of Paper* he insisted that I should take the number one dressing room at the Empire. This had always been his as Mr. Frohman's leading star. In his absence Maude Adams and I had used it, but the idea of occupying it when he was in the play would never have entered my head. When I protested, he said, "Nonsense, it's where you belong."

I like to remember his last tour. It was an all-star production of *Trelawny of the Wells,* and all the way across the country Uncle Jack, who was well past seventy, and Mrs. Whiffen, who was well over eighty, were the only two members of the company who never once made any complaint, although some of the younger stars made a great many.

It was characteristic of him that all through that tour when he was suffering from arthritis so that every motion caused him intense pain, he somehow managed to make his acting seem as effortless as ever. Out of consideration for the rest of the company, to some of whom closing the play might have involved hardship, he kept on acting until it was physically impossible for him to go on.

I like to remember, too, his last words, spoken to his daughter Bee just before he died: "Take care of the nurses."

After *The Scrap of Paper* I went to Mamaroneck for the summer. It is hard to believe now, that it could have begun so well; that, until almost half of it was spent, most of us were happy people, living in a happy world.

The last few bright days seem now to have been the brightest ones. Russell and I spent some of them at Forest Hills, watching the unforgettable Davis Cup matches in which Anthony Wilding and Norman Brookes played against McLaughlin, first of the cannonballs, and Norris Williams, who managed to be almost as good as the best of the smashing, rough-and-tumble players and yet to play the most perfectly gentlemanly game I ever saw on a court.

I think that in my memory those velvet courts perhaps may seem more smoothly green than they really were, that on them the white-flanneled figures—so different from the shorts and singlets of today—may seem to move more swiftly and gracefully than they actually did, that the colors in the stands may seem more gaily brilliant than they were and the sky more brightly blue, because I remember all these things now against the blackness of the shadow that was still invisible, although so near.

The summer into which that First World War exploded seems now to have been so utterly unlike any later summer that the world has known or can ever know again! A summer of peace and leisure and decency, while life still moved afoot, unhurrying, when tomorrow, or the next day or the next was soon enough for news, when the sky, all the way to the stars, was clear and still and clean, when we could still hold to our faith that men had risen forever above the beastliness of beasts, when we had yet to learn, unbelieving, how far below that beastliness men could still descend.

For me, with all my ties to England, the war began, not three years later, but on that midsummer day when the Germans struck. In the "First Hundred Thousand" sent out to die, so bravely and to so little gain, by a chivalry for which the new world had no use, were nearly all the young men I had known and many boys like the Grenfells, whom I was still thinking of as children. Julian Grenfell left Oxford to go to the front, where he wrote, in his poem "Into Battle,"

> The Blackbird sings to him, "Brother, brother,
>   If this be the last song you shall sing,
> Sing well, for you may not sing another;
>   Brother, sing!"

Julian did not sing another. He sent the poem to his mother the day before he was killed. A letter from him, and one from Willie, who had been still at Eton, reached me after they both were dead.

It was the beginning, for me, of four years of dreading to hear news, of slowly learning to face the fact that men who had once seemed as human as the men I knew could do unspeakable things not only in anger to other men but in cold blood to helpless children, and to women, even to such a woman as Edith Cavell.

Dick Davis went as a war correspondent to Brussels, and there, from a window in the U.S. Embassy, watched the Germans entering the city and wrote his famous report:

We saw it first in the warm summer sunshine, later under the glare of electric lamps, hours later in the grey of the morning. . . .

For three days and three nights through Brussels it roared and rumbled, a cataract of molten lead. The infantry marched singing, with their iron shod boots beating out the time. In each regiment there were 2,000 men and at the same instant, in perfect unison, 2,000 iron brogans struck the granite street. The Uhlans followed. . . . For three days and three nights the column of grey, with fifty thousand bayonets and fifty thousand lances, with grey transport wagons, grey ammunition carts, grey ambulances, grey cannon, like a river of steel cut Brussels in two.

Dick was dead in April of 1916. Another correspondent, Herbert Bayard Swope, from Berlin sent to the New York *World* and St. Louis *Post-Dispatch* exclusive dispatches about the sinking of battleships by the German U-boats and, in a year of much brilliant newswriting, was awarded a Pulitzer prize for the best reporting of 1917.

Uncle Sidney's son, Sidney Rankin Drew, joined the Lafayette Esquadrille before we went into the First World War and was shot down in flames. Uncle Sidney never got over his death. After the war Uncle Sidney's second wife, Lucille McVey, went to France to look for Sidney's grave. After a great deal of trouble, she found a little garden with a picket fence around it covered with flowers and a cross saying:

SIDNEY RANKIN DREW, HERO.

He had fallen behind the lines, and it was the Germans who had paid him that tribute. She felt she could do no better, so left it there.

Russell went, almost at once, to drive an ambulance in France. I stayed at home until, leaving the children in the care of the nurses and their governess, Miss Jackson, I went on tour in *The Shadow* before opening at the Empire in January.

The Shadow was a gorgeous drama from the French, written originally for Réjane, but the war had stopped its production in Paris. I don't know that it has ever been done there. It was a tremendously interesting part for me. In the first act I was a paralytic and sat motionless in a chair for thirty-five minutes. I thought it would be very difficult to do but, curiously enough, I never even had to practice not moving. As soon as I got into that chair and the cover was laid over my knees and hands, the curtain went up and the play began; I don't think I could have moved if I had wanted to. Bruce McRae came back to me for this play, which pleased me very much, as I always entertained great affection for him.

The Shadow was very sad, but it had moments of great exaltation and beauty. Many people told me they liked me better in it than anything they had seen me in. I always wanted to do it again sometime.

The next piece was a decided contrast to what I had done before—an American play from the stories of Edna Ferber, called *Our Mrs. McChesney*, a comedy with a "mother note" in it. It was a great success everywhere except Chicago. They preferred me there in serious plays. Boston, which is generally thought to be the most highbrow of our cities, loved it and we could have gone on there indefinitely, I think, but it was June and the season was over.

During rehearsals and the run of *Mrs. McChesney* I got to know Edna Ferber and liked and admired her tremendously. She gave a supper party one night at which I sat next to

William Allen White. I found Mr. White to be one of the most delightful persons I had ever met. He amused us all by telling of his experiences on a recent trip to England.

I remember that he told us his sense of convention had been shocked at a weekend party in the country by the fact that he and his wife were put in separate rooms. He also received another shock in the morning when the maid unceremoniously entered his room with a cup of tea and opened his curtains. He talked of many interesting and absorbing things. I liked him very much and always wanted to see him again.

In April when I was playing in Boston I heard that Mr. Frohman had decided to go to London, much against everybody's wishes. I was about to go to Chicago and knew that I wouldn't have a chance to say good-by to him unless I went to New York before he left. So I went down on Sunday night and early on Monday morning I went in to see him.

He said, "What are you doing here, Ethel?"

(He called me Ethel, but I always called him Mr. Frohman.)

I said, "I thought I would come down to say good-by."

He said, "They don't want me to go on this boat. I had a funny message from von Papen and Captain Boy-Ed, telling me not to go on the *Lusitania*."

I said, "Why go then?"

He said, "Nonsense, of course I'll go."

When he said good-by, he leaned over and kissed me on the cheek. He had never done that before. All the way back to Boston on the train I was worried, but I knew that nothing could happen to Mr. Frohman.

I went to Chicago. During the run of *Mrs. McChesney*

there a friend of mine gave a luncheon at her house for Elsie Ferguson, who was playing in town at the same time. I was called to the telephone by Cecil Clark Davis, who said she had heard the most terrible news but it had not been confirmed, yet everybody was afraid it was true. I asked her what it was, and she said that the *Lusitania* had been sunk with all on board.

When I went back to the table, they all wanted to know what it was that made me look so utterly downcast and I told them.

I remember Elsie Ferguson and myself just looking at each other and saying, "Mr. Frohman . . . Mr. Frohman . . ."

It was not long before Joe Patterson telephoned me and we had to accept the terrible fact that Mr. Frohman had gone. For many years he had been my very best friend. He had taken the place of parents and I had gone to him with not only my theater troubles, but all my troubles. He had always been understanding and wonderful.

Nothing was ever quite the same after that for me.

I shall always remember him with love. A wonderful, golden man.

Russell came back from France because he did not care to be called an *embusqué* by men who were facing no more danger than ambulance drivers, and by some who were facing far less. He went to Plattsburg, in the summer, for a month of military training, and the children and I stayed at Mamaroneck.

It was at such periods that my children and I would have uninterrupted good times—almost happy in spite of the darkening shadow of the war. The children all loved the theater, taking a perfectly natural interest in it, but I tried never to influence them for or against going on the stage. When Sister played in a school production of *Ivanhoe* I didn't help her or know anything about it until the performance, in which she was delightful, natural and at home and aloof from the audience. Sammy played in school theatricals, too.

Once when Jackie, about six, was home for an Easter vacation a friend asked him one day, "Well, Jackie, are you going to be an actor?"

He said, "Oh, I don't know. Maybe I might be a comedy."

They grew up just like other children—fighting like the dickens sometimes, then making up, very happy and loving each other very much.

When Russell went to Palm Beach for the winter, I brought the children in to be with me at the Netherlands, while I made my first motion picture at the studio just across the Park. Metro Corporation had offered me very enticing terms to do eight pictures. I thought it was a wise thing for me to do, as things were at the time, and it was pleasant dough and no traveling.

Sammy went to St. Bernard's School and Sister to kindergarten, and with Jackie old enough now to sit solidly in a saddle, they all went riding in the Park on every sunny day. The great black admiral of the fleet who was the doorman at the Netherlands used to see them safely across the street and onto the path.

I spent all that season in pictures. I didn't like them very much, and was very glad when the year was over. In one of these pictures I was a Russian princess and there was a scene in which my sleigh broke down in the snow. A lot of extras had been hired, nearly all Russians who wore funny fur caps and beards, real beards, to stand around in this scene. No one talked to them because they seemed to speak only Russian.

Years later when I was going through some photographs at Mamaroneck I came across one of the stills from this picture. As I looked at the group of peasants, one face was unmistakable.

I said, "That's Trotsky!"

And there he was. It was long after the Russian revolution, Trotsky was dead—murdered—but it was known that he had spent several years in New York, working at various things including an occasional day on the movie lot, earning a capitalistic $5—and glad to get it.

The last scenes of my last picture were photographed at Jacksonville. Afterward, I went to Palm Beach, where I spent the two most miserable weeks of my life.

I came north just as, at last, America entered the war. There was no room for Russell at Plattsburg but he got his commission at Watertown and was in France till the war was over.

The Stage Women's War Relief was instrumental in getting Mr. Al Hayman to let them have the Empire Theatre so as to produce three Barrie plays, *The New Word*, *Old Friends* and *The Old Lady Shows Her Medals*. *Old Friends* was not successful but, of course, *The New Word* and *The Old Lady Shows Her Medals* were enormously so.

In spite of the beauty of these performances, the houses

were not very good and one night at Mamaroneck it occurred to me that they might like to put *The Twelve Pound Look* on the bill instead of the unsuccessful one-act piece. I was sure that it would draw the people in, and that they would enjoy the other plays after they got there.

So I went straight to the telephone and called up Mr. Hayman at his house and suggested the plan to him. He didn't seem to understand at first that I wanted to play for nothing, but when he did he was delighted. We got four or five good weeks out of that and made some money for charity. That was the beginning of my war work. I was never able to do very much, but I did all that I could, as we all did.

Later in the fall I played *The Twelve Pound Look* in vaudeville. Mr. Hayman had promised that I could have a repertory season at the Empire, a thing that I had always longed to have, and on the day before Christmas I opened at the Empire in *The Lady of the Camellias*. Ned Sheldon had written a new and lovely version of the story, taking it directly from the book. I have always thought it most beautiful. We did it in the costumes of the period in which it was written, as I have always felt it should be done.

The play begins after Marguerite's death, with all the great ladies of France buying her belongings at an auction in her apartment. When the sale is over, Armand bribes the concierge to let him spend the night in the apartment. He cries out, "Marguerite, my love, come back to me," the scene blacks out and the story is told as a dream in Armand's mind.

At the end, after I died and the scene blacked out again, everybody in the audience was blowing his nose. Marie

Louise Wanamaker and Mary Brown Warburton, her cousin, used to come to every matinee and cry and cry. They would bring men's handkerchiefs and pin them to backs of the seats in front of them to dry. Sometimes when they were at the Follies with young men, they would say suddenly, "Oh, let's go and see her die!" And they'd fly over to the Empire Theatre dragging the unwilling young men with them.

"Oh, let's go and see her die" became another of the family wheezes.

I don't think I have ever played a part that I really loved so much. I did it about three months and then produced a light modern comedy by R. C. Carton called *The Off Chance*. It was a great contrast and a most amusing play. Eva Le Gallienne was very young and gave the most beautiful performance.

The Off Chance seemed to offer so much promise of a long tour that, instead of going on tour with it for what was left of the season when its New York run ended in May, I decided to save it for the fall and finished the season in New York with *Belinda*, a light, delightful bit of fluff by A. A. Milne.

During this repertory season there were many benefits and pageants given for various war charities. The first one was the big pageant of all the Allies at Madison Square Garden in which I was devastated Belgium, with sufficient effect to make me go on being devastated Belgium more or less indefinitely until the end of the war.

I was called on constantly. It was very difficult for me to know what to do, as I had always had a horror of recitations and was firmly convinced no power under heaven could make me recite. For any charitable event, I always had appeared in one-act plays or in single scenes from long plays. Now that I was faced with my war work, I had to learn to recite.

It is impossible to convey the abject terror I was in the first time I stepped upon the stage alone, as myself, to utter. It was on the occasion of a benefit for the Red Cross at the Metropolitan Opera House.

It was almost entirely a musical program, orchestral and choruses, and above all, Caruso. I was the only other soloist, which naturally intensified my panic. The poem was "The Battle Hymn of the Republic." I had always known it vaguely—in fact, that was the only way I did know it—very vaguely! I had studied it, but I had little confidence in my memory under the terrifying circumstances, so I asked my brother Lionel to go into the prompter's box, which is immediately in front of where I was to stand during the ordeal.

My feelings when coming through the famous golden curtains of the Metropolitan and facing a mammoth audience are indescribable. I began with quite a dash, a little like going over the top, but keeping firmly in my mind at the time that if I should forget, there at my very feet was my brother Lionel with the poem in his hand, ready for the worst.

Just before the last verse, the worst happened; my mind suddenly became a hideous blank. There was a pause; I suppose it was really only an instant, but it seemed to me a million years. Suddenly a sound came to me from the prompter's box; it was Lionel trying to give me the lines. I heard nothing but what sounded like the muffled roar of a lion. He repeated it several times, but it never meant anything to me except the strange cry of some jungle beast. Finally, just as the words had gone, they came back to me and I finished the poem amid thunderous applause.

After the performance John McCormack came back to congratulate me. He spoke about how wonderful my voice had sounded and how particularly marvelous was the great change I made just before the last verse. He had thought that only a singer could produce such an amazing effect. Thus is bravery rewarded!

The next thing I did in this line was at the stadium of the New York City College, a place holding forty thousand people. I was to recite Zoë Akin's "Ode to the Allies." A glorious thing, but it was very long and this time I had it largely and blackly inscribed on a scroll of parchment, which I held firmly grasped in my two hands. I was, of course, as nervous as ever, but got a certain amount of confidence holding tightly to the parchment before going onto the platform. It was at night but the platform was well lighted, so I knew I could see to read. But what I didn't know or expect was that I would be flooded with enormous spotlights that I would have to look at while bowing. As they kindly applauded my entrance, it was a little like looking at the noonday sun. I was completely blinded so, when I looked at the parchment to begin my ode, I saw nothing whatsoever for what seemed a space of eternity. I have always hoped that the largeness of the place and the vast numbers of people made that time seem shorter. At any rate, it was all right, and I had again done a little of my "bit."

During that summer, after the frightening weeks in the spring when the Germans had seemed to be breaking through our line, it was possible at least to begin believing that the war was going to be won and even that the winning might be worth the dreadful price that the casualty lists told us it was costing. It was possible to hold to that faith through the first months that followed the hysteria of triumph. It seems incredible now that we should actually have believed that there would never be another war, but it was good, blessedly good, to believe it, and for me it is good to remember now that once I could and did believe it.

VI

It's All Right. We've Won.

We've Won!

At the Algonquin one night when I was having supper with Uncle Jack and Aunt Dodo after the theater, Jobyna Howland came to our table and spoke to us. There was a girl with her whom I didn't know. As they passed the table, the other girl said to me, in a curious accent, "I've written a play for you."

After they had gone I turned to Uncle Jack and said, "Who was the Polish girl with Joby?"

Uncle Jack said, "I think her name is Zoë Akins."

Not long afterward Alf Hayman gave me two acts of a play and said, "Read this."

I got into my car to drive out to Mamaroneck and began reading it. By the time I reached New Rochelle I had finished the two acts. I tapped on the glass and said, "Britt, go right back to the Empire Theatre," which we did.

I said to Hayman, "Where is the third act? Get it as quickly as possible. I've got to do this play."

It was *Déclassée*, the play that the "Polish" girl had spoken to me about. It turned out that she came from St. Louis and that her accent, though completely natural, was a peculiar thing of her own.

That summer Russell and I went to Toledo to see the Dempsey-Willard fight. Dempsey had been discovered by Otto Floto, whom Jack and I had met when we were playing *Sunday* in Denver where he was sports editor of the Denver *Post*. As we were starting for Toledo, I received a telegram from Otto saying, "Tell Russell to put his shirt on Dempsey."

So of course Russell bet on Willard. (I remember him

saying, "Ten men couldn't beat him!") and so did everybody else except me.

I remember how frightening-looking Jack Dempsey was before the fight, his black beard showing through his skin. He was wearing a scapular and he kept crossing himself. Willard looked like an unscalable mountain. The fight was almost over with the first punch. It was horrible, brutal, terrible. I never wanted to see another heavyweight fight after that. Everyone stood up all the way through the fight after the first round. I was shaking all over. I didn't look at it very much.

After the fight Russell and I were walking behind the grandstand to find the car, and we saw Willard, just sort of stumbling along with a towel wrapped around his head. Nobody was with him, no seconds, no friends, just two little urchins, looking up at him as if they were looking up at the top of Mt. Everest. He kept mumbling, "Isn't it awful? Isn't it awful?"

Altogether a pretty harrowing day!

On the way back the news got around the train that I had picked Dempsey, and Bill McGeehan and Grantland Rice and other newspapermen came into the drawing room to ask me about it. "Why did you pick Dempsey? Will you write a story for us?"

I said, "I couldn't do that."

"But why did you pick this unknown, Dempsey?"

"Because Otto Floto told me to," I said. "He discovered him in a mining camp somewhere and telegraphed me to bet on him. I knew he wouldn't have sent me that telegram unless he was awfully sure."

In August, as I had been doing ever since I had stopped going to England for the summer, I went down to White Sulphur Springs for two weeks of taking the baths and playing golf. I loved the old hotel there with the ballroom floor that had been intentionally designed to wave up and down as one danced on it, but there is a new hotel now and the waving floor is gone.

I shall always remember one thing that happened at White Sulphur—the time when Tom Payne, a delightful man from Atlanta, came up to me and said, "The next time you're down at the golf course I wish you'd watch a young protégé of mine play."

I was playing every day but I made a special trip to see Mr. Payne's prodigy, a boy about fourteen. His name was Bobby Jones.

When I went down to the Springs this year, Zoë Akins had finished the third act of *Déclassée* and I knew that I had a wonderful play for the fall. I expected to begin rehearsals in it as soon as I came back to New York.

But when I came back and went to see my cousin Georgie, who was living on Forty-fifth Street, there was such a mass of people in the street that the car couldn't get through, and I had to get out and walk to Georgie's apartment. I asked her what all those people were doing, and she said, "Don't you know? It's the actors' strike."

"Strike," I said, "what for?"

I hadn't been reading the papers and didn't know, until Georgie told me, that nearly all the theaters were closed, that nearly all actors, including all but a few of the leading ones, were on strike.

I, who had only the most wonderful treatment from Mr. Frohman and his successor, Alf Hayman, had no grievances of my own. It was something of a shock when Georgie explained the grievances that had brought about the strike, to find out that the members of the Actors Equity were asking for so very, very little, for things that, it seemed to me, should in common decency have been theirs without the asking. It seemed a shameful thing that people should have to go on strike to gain assurance that they would be brought back to New York when a play closed on tour instead of being left penniless in Texas, that they should be offering to rehearse without pay for four weeks—six weeks for musicals —and after that to go on rehearsing for half pay!

I suddenly knew that I had to do something about it. "I ought to belong to Equity," I said.

Georgie stared at me, "You damn fool," she said, "you're a life member."

I suppose someone sometime had told me about something I ought to belong to, put a card in front of me, and I must have signed it and paid my $100. I didn't remember doing it, but I was very, very glad to find that I had done it. (Luckily for me it was in that happier era that I stopped signing things without looking at them!)

Georgie said, "You should go and show yourself at headquarters and be there, as everyone else is."

She spent a long time trying to convince me that my presence at headquarters would be of importance—but without success. However, I started for headquarters with her eventually, merely because I thought it would please her and because she seemed so anxious for it.

We got out of Georgie's apartment and the crowd sort of

gathered me up and swept me along. It was a little terrifying; I kept thinking that things like this must have happened during the French Revolution. By the time we reached the brownstone house that was headquarters the crowd had caught sight of me and suddenly a sound went up—a great shout that seemed to come from the souls of these people who were my people. It left me trembling from head to foot with a feeling of exaltation and happiness. The thought that they felt I could be of some use to them made me prouder than mere words can tell.

I was practically carried along up the steps and into the house. I found myself up on a table. People were crying and kissing my hands and even the hem of my dress and saying, "It's all right. We've won. We've won!"

I had a moment's feeling of being a Joan of Arc. It was all terribly moving and exciting. All I said was, "I'm with you, whatever it is," and suddenly everything seemed to become organized as if all that had been needed was somebody to lead.

Uncle Jack, who of course was with the actors, was in East Hampton, and after talking with him I wrote a letter for him to read at a meeting of Equity. It said:

> While my entire theatrical career has been associated with but one management from whom I have received only fairness and consideration, I feel that the traditions of my family and my personal predilections ally me, logically and irremediably, with the members of my profession in the Actors Equity Association.

Uncle Jack also announced that both Lionel and Jack, who were out of town, had asked him to notify the meeting that they were with the strikers.

Of course I was present at all the meetings and gave the *New York Times* a statement about the effect of the strike on the strikers. It was this aspect of the strike that had most deeply touched me. For the first time in the history of such conflicts people with no grievances, with nothing whatever to gain and a great deal to lose, had gone on strike as a matter of principle and principle only, with no selfish interest to serve, seeking only justice for fellow workers unable to secure it for themselves.

I wrote:

I have never seen faces change so. Men and women who never seemed to have a thought for anything but their own advantage are absolutely forgetting themselves. Of course it changes them. They are working for others and for a principle and there is a look of devotion on their faces.

The statement went on to explain that it was the commercialization of the theater that had caused the strike.

People understand, I think, that all my experience under one management has been a happy one. Mr. Frohman never made a contract and always kept his word. The time when I began work and the time before that when the older members of my family were acting, was the day of the individual manager. As a business the theater wasn't so well developed. There were plenty of practical disadvantages, but at least there was a courtesy and a sense of high tradition.

Actors of that day were the ladies and gentlemen of the company. They were addressed accordingly. Now it is, "hey, you!"

The change began with the great combinations of managers. From that time on, making more money, at any sacrifice of standards, has been their one end. Of course, there are exceptions. It is the general tendency that I'm talking about. A good many managers appear to think they are simply merchants and the actors are their stock in trade. When they think more money can be made that way, they put on plays that the best of the profession are ashamed of. . . . Of all the childish things that have been said against us, the funniest is that the actors are forgetting the dignity of their art!

Dignity! Think of it! Some of our own people have left us with that word for an excuse! I can't understand them. It's character that gives people dignity. And I don't know any better proof of character than standing firm for a principle. . . .

This experience is good for us. It is teaching us to depend on ourselves. And, even better, to depend upon each other. The actor is growing up. He is becoming social.

All we are working for is democracy in the theatre, justice, equality, truth. I have never thought of leaving the cause. I believe with my whole heart that it is right. But if I felt less conviction than I do, I would not leave. These are my people.

Mr. Robert Cole of the *Times,* to whom I had given the statement, made this comment of his own about the interview. I am quoting it because what it says about me and my attitude is just as true, and perhaps truer, about so many of the other men and women who made that fight and helped to win it.

Perhaps the most curious fact of the revolution is the presence in the crowd of the traditional aristocrat, whose interest would seem to lie with the establishment. This woman, who speaks so earnestly for the obscure actor, is an aristocrat of the stage. Those who saw her in Barrie's "Twelve-Pound Look," however, find nothing strange in her present attitude. If ever she seemed to be playing herself, speaking out of her heart from the stage, it was in the character of the woman who left every comfort to become a poor stenographer, because she hated the world where material success was everything, where invisible realities were despised. In the same accents today she despises the man who can see nothing but money in the theatre.

A few actors, some of them important, were against us. They formed an organization that they called Actors' Fidelity and that we called the Fidoes. They set up Janet Beecher as a kind of figurehead and kept referring to her as "the purest woman on the American stage." Lionel said, "What does that mean? It sounds like the freshest egg in Jersey. You're either pure or not." And it didn't prove to be a very good slogan.

I received various messages from Mr. Hayman during this time, commanding me and begging me to come to rehearsals which, of course, was absurd because we were right in the midst of the strike and if I had gone to rehearsals it would have been the same thing as playing. It was simply impossible. Of course he must have realized it, but he pretended not to. He said it wasn't like playing and he didn't see why I couldn't rehearse. He really became very, very angry.

One day when I went to see him to explain the reasons why I could not go to rehearsals, he said he could not hold them up any longer and had cabled for Mrs. Patrick Campbell to come over and play my part. I said I was sure she would be very good.

Of course, he had not cabled, but I didn't know it, and I just took it for granted that I had lost it.

He and the other managers called us contract breakers and

everything else they could think of. Some of them sued us for fantastic amounts and got injunctions against us, but more and more theaters kept closing until almost none were open.

When the strikers began to get hungry—and being actors, a lot of them already were—we organized three weeks of benefit performances at the Lexington Avenue Opera House. We had closed all the theaters in New York with the exception of this one and so, naturally, the public flocked to it. We felt that they flocked to it in an enormously sympathetic way.

The first week I did the second act of *The Lady of the Camellias* with my brother Lionel as a superb Père Duval and ConwayTearle as Armand. When I made my entrance the opening night the audience gave me a reception that lasted for three minutes. Alexander Woollcott wrote:

The rip-roaring and delightful entertainment staged lavishly by the rebel players before huge audiences over Lexington Avenue way reveals Ethel Barrymore, playing beautifully as Marguerite Gautier in "The Lady of the Camellias." She can even step into a program of Eddie Foys and Eddie Cantors and bestow on all the evening a certain unforgettable radiance. It was curious to witness how instantly the strains of the "Plaisir d'Amour" hushed the hilarious audience to the mood for an old romance incomparably played. And Miss Barrymore's voice! But then how can a humdrum day-by-day reviewer of dramatic entertainment hope to describe that enchantment. It would be like measuring the music of a purling brook and that calls for a poet.

(I quote those extravagances about my voice because they reminded me, when I read them, of the time when I decided that something must be done about it. Although I was being mimicked everywhere on land and sea, I was always worried about my voice because it was so very low and had that sort of breathless quality. I heard of a singing teacher named

ETHEL BARRYMORE WINS SPEECH PRIZE

Actress Receives Gold Medal From Academy of Arts and Letters for Stage Work

By SAM ZOLOTOW

Through the years all sorts of decorations have been showered on Ethel Barrymore for distinguished service as an actress. (Pay no attention to the Hollywood phase.) To her long list of acting tributes add a fourteen-carat gold medal for "beauty of speech on the American stage," the 1946 award by the American Academy of Arts and Letters. Previous winners have been such notables as Otis Skinner, Julia Marlowe, George Arliss, Lynn Fontanne and Eva Le Gallienne.

Academy Award for "beauty of speech" as reported in the *New York Times* on April 10, 1946, proves Miss Barrymore's early worries unfounded.

Mrs. Morris and thought that she might help me. So, for some time, I stopped almost every day on my way to the theater and had a singing lesson from her. Curiously enough it turned out that my singing voice was a high soprano. I learned several dramatic soprano roles, and there is no doubt that it helped me in such ways as voice production and breath control. But I am afraid that God meant me to have this voice and that I'm stuck with it.)

Almost every great figure of the contemporary stage was on those Equity benefit programs. I remember that Ed Wynn had to sit in the audience because the Shuberts had gotten an injunction forbidding him to appear on the stage. Suddenly a spotlight was turned on him, and he stood up and without moving a step was at his humorous best, with the whole audience cheering him.

The spirit of the players was wonderful. The biggest stars were exactly like the chorus players. If they were told to go up eight flights of stairs to the dressing rooms and then go onto the stage to speak one line, they were only too delighted to do it. That's why the benefits were always so successful. The enthusiasm of the players for the cause went right across to the audience and we got immediate return from them—just like a ball being tossed back and forth; you threw it out to them and they threw it back to you; regular team play. I am sure that is what helped us all to stand together.

The second week Conway Tearle and I played the balcony scene from *Romeo and Juliet* and the list of names on the program was even more impressive than that of the week before. We also gave a ball at the Astor where Uncle Jack and I led the grand march. Douglas Fairbanks and many other motion-picture stars purchased boxes to make it clear that they were on our side in the strike. The ball netted $7,000 for the strike fund and those of the strikers who could afford to contribute added $20,000 more.

It was evident that the public was on our side and the

opposition began to crumble. Early in September the managers gave in on all points, even agreeing—think of it—to pay full salary after four weeks of free rehearsals, instead of the half pay we had originally asked for.

I shall never forget the way in which the strike came to an end. Representatives from both sides were assembled. I was one of the people appointed to sign the five-year agreement between the managers and the Equity Association. I was up all night waiting for the lawyers, managers and players to get the papers ready, to "come across," as it were, to accept the inevitable situation and to sign. When we left the room about three o'clock in the morning, the strike was over and settled and we all went back to work.

I began rehearsing for *Déclassée,* and nothing was said about Mrs. Campbell or about the strike. It wasn't to be expected, though, that after such a bitter quarrel nobody should harbor any ill feelings, especially those who were on the losing side. All the time we were rehearsing *Déclassée* Alf Hayman made it very clear that he hadn't forgiven me. He sulked and grumbled, but I always pretended I didn't notice any of his ill humor.

We had nothing new for the play—repainted scenery and furniture from the storehouse. In the first act, I remember, we required a large sofa but Mr. Hayman, in his mood, did not feel that he wanted to get one. I insisted that we must have a sofa instead of the cane bench that went with the set of furniture wished upon us from the storehouse.

At that time "Charles Frohman, Incorporated" had become affiliated with the Famous Players and I found it very hard to talk to Mr. Hayman about anything. He was very "strikey." So I went to Mr. Lasky, or one of those at the head of the moving-picture office, to speak about the sofa, and I was told to go ahead and get it. The thought of those great magnates sitting there and saying, "Go ahead and get your sofa—you must have it," always amused me, for I paid for it, and neither Mr. Hayman nor Mr. Lasky ever paid me back. In the old days Mr. Hayman would have bought eight sofas for me, and Mr. Frohman, of course, never would have thought much about the matter—if I had asked him. Nevertheless I got the sofa and it made the scene because it was new and very beautiful.

The first-night audience in New York went enthusiastically insane, but all Mr. Hayman would say, after the curtain, was: "Well, it may be all right—if that audience is on the level."

In the morning, though, all the critics were even more enthusiastic than the audience had been. Heywood Broun ended his notice with "Beg, borrow, or steal, but get to the Empire Theatre!" The public seemed bent on following this advice. Firemen had to be called on to help the police handle the crowds in front of the theater and Mr. Hayman was at last convinced. He opened a second box office in which he helped in person to sell tickets.

But almost at once the critics began trying to take back those wildly enthusiastic reviews, and they kept on trying for the next three years. I have always thought that their change of attitude and their efforts to be funny at Zoë Akins' expense originated at the Round Table at the Algonquin where the wisecrack often passed for wit. In spite of their efforts, of which I am bound to say the general public seemed completely unaware, the play kept on being a colossal success.

We played it for nine months before going on tour with it; every seat for every performance was bought up and people stood at every performance.

But, ironically, while that success was at its height, I had at last to face the realization that there was no hope of making a success of my marriage.

After eleven years of trying my best to save it, I went to see Cardinal Hayes and told him that I was going to get a divorce. He said, "Oh, no, you can't do that." But after a long discussion, he said, "All right but you mustn't marry again."

I remember that I found no difficulty in reassuring him. It never entered my head to marry again. My divorce is merely legal. It was granted in Rhode Island, quietly and without opposition, on the grounds of desertion and non-support.

I think that both my brothers and I were born under a dark star so that there was no such thing for us as enduring happiness. Perhaps it is an inheritance; I think now that the time when my mother and father were saying good-by to each other on the boat and I heard her begging him not to forget her was the beginning, although I did not know it then, of my awareness of the dark star.

I do not want to blame anybody for the failure of my marriage, except, perhaps, that star.

Although I didn't succeed in saving the marriage itself, I did manage to save some of the pieces. Under the terms of

the divorce, Russell had the right to see the children and I
thought it was better for us to see them together. When he
was not in Palm Beach, he came to dinner once a week at
our house or took us out to a restaurant. He always came to
dinner on Thanksgiving Day and on Christmas whenever I
was playing somewhere nearby and had the children with
me for their holidays. Always taking the children with us,
we kept on going to baseball games, and when the boys were
old enough, to boxing matches at Madison Square Garden.
Our relations have remained on this amicable footing, so
much so that years later, before their marriage, Russell asked
me to dinner at the Metropolitan Club to meet his present
wife, whom I thought perfectly charming. She had a small
son and afterward Russell asked me had I ever known an
eleven-year-old boy.

I said, "Yes. Two."

He said, "Who?"

I said, "Sammy and Jackie Colt."

He had forgotten all about them.

I think Colonel Colt, who was always kind and generous
to me and the children, felt very unhappy about the divorce.
To this day, whenever I am anywhere near Providence, all
Colts and De Wolfes make a point of telephoning "Cousin
Ethel."

Déclassée ran on and on, all through that season and the
next and, except when it was interrupted by the only serious
illness I had had, through the next.

I was playing it in Cincinnati. One night when I was sitting on the sofa in the last act, just before the time for me to
go out and get run over, I suddenly couldn't move. Some-

thing like a bolt of lightning had struck my back. As I was
saying my lines, I kept thinking that I would not be able to
get up to get off the stage; I don't know how, but I did get
off. The pain was now in my knee. It was fortunate that the
play called for me to be carried back onto the stage by a
strong young footman and placed on a sofa, where I proceeded, gracefully, to die.

(Incidentally, what a beautifully written scene that was
—'Oh, to be in England now that April's there!')

After the curtain they called a cab, took me to the hotel
and sent for a doctor. By the time he got there the pain had
gone to my hand and I was making the most terrible sounds
from the agony. The doctor said it sounded like fugitive
arthritis. The next thing I knew I was in an ambulance on
my way to Christ's Hospital, where I spent the next four
months.

I sent for the children and their nurse and put them in
the Sinton Hotel and they were brought to see me for a few
minutes whenever I was well enough.

When I got back to New York I was met by Dr. Danforth
and Uncle Jack and Jack and taken straight from the train
to the Flower Hospital, where they found the cause of all
the anguish—a streptococcic infection lodged in my tonsils
—they had to come out. The operation was postponed and
postponed until I was strong enough to stand it. It was a
major operation; it took an hour and a quarter.

The arthritis left me with a bad finger. When they took
me down to the operating room I asked them if I could ever
play the piano again, and they said it would be impossible.
This made me feel dreadful—but I can!

While I was in the Flower Hospital my brother Jack came to see me and show me a new play called *Clair de Lune* written by Michael Strange, his second wife. He wanted me to play the queen in it. He had gone to see Mr. Hayman about it and he was much interested in the idea of the two Barrymores appearing in a play by Jack's wife.

After such an illness as I had gone through it was naturally impossible for me to go back to such a heavy role as that in *Déclassée*—nor could I have traveled. The responsibility of the whole thing would have been too much for me. The part in *Clair de Lune* was short, and I told Jack that if I didn't die, I would play it. There was at one time great doubt as to whether I would get better.

During the last few weeks that I was in the hospital Jack came to me with plates for costumes, scenery, etc., and I had never seen him so interested in anything connected with the theater as in these preparations. As soon as I got out of the hospital we began rehearsals and shortly afterward produced the play.

The critics castigated it so severely that Jack was infuriated. He came to my dressing room after the second night's performance and announced that he was going out in front of the curtain and make a speech in answer to the critics. I did everything I could to dissuade him, and at last I called up Lionel in Port Jefferson—the telephone that I had installed when Sammy was born was very useful—and between us, meanwhile keeping the audience waiting for the curtain to go up, we persuaded Jack not to make the speech. But we did not succeed in preventing him from sending it in letter form to the *Times* and the *Tribune*.

When *Clair de Lune* closed, I was well enough to go back to *Déclassée*, in which I kept on playing for another year.

It was during that year that we played it in Washington, and President Wilson sat in a box at a matinee. This was after his stroke, and to make it as easy as possible for him to leave the theater, his car had been parked in the alley in front of the stage door. To reach it he had to go right past the door of my dressing room. He was leaning on a little colored man. He had been crying and his eyes were shining. He said, "It was beautiful, my dear. It was beautiful."

That was the last time I ever spoke with Mr. Wilson, but not the last time that I saw him. A year or so later, when I was playing *The Twelve Pound Look* at Keith's in Washington, he was in the audience. As I did not have to go on the stage until about 9:30, I had gone to dinner at the Longworths' before leaving for the theater and had promised to come back after the performance. But when I went out there was a solid mass of people for blocks around the theater, all waiting to see Mr. Wilson come out, although he had been out of office for some time. I was deeply moved and naturally I waited until he had left. By then it was so late that I hesitated to go back to the Longworths', but I did. Alice asked me where I'd been. I said, "I couldn't get out of the theater any sooner because there was such a terrific crowd around it waiting to see Mr. Wilson leave."

She said, *"Who?"*

When I told her, she wouldn't believe me. She hated Wilson so bitterly that she simply couldn't believe a great crowd had waited just to see him pass.

By the time *Déclassée* ended its three-year run all the children were in school. Sammy had gone from St. Bernard's, in New York, to Andover, but after going to see him when I was playing in Boston I could not feel right about leaving him there. He seemed too young for such a big school. So next year, I sent him to Canterbury, in New Milford, Connecticut, which had been established by rich Catholics like the Ryans, Bradys and Mackeys, an excellent school run by laymen and probably the most expensive school on earth.

Jackie went first to Fay School, in Massachusetts, and then to Portsmouth Priory at Newport, run by the Benedictines. Its headmaster was Dr. Diamond, a convert who had previously been head of St. George's School.

Sister had gone to the Lenox School in New York, but I dreaded sending her to one of the fashionable schools there, and when I was going on a long tour, I suddenly thought of the only right place in the world for her—the convent, my convent. It was the same place it had been when I was there, with some of the same sisters, among them Sister Julie de St. Esprit, who had been mistress of boarders when I was there, and was now head of the Children of Mary, the alumnae. Sister adored the convent and got the most amazing marks, so high that I asked the Sister Superior how it was possible.

"My dear," she said, "we have to give them what they make."

It was a great relief to me, knowing every hour of the day that she was doing exactly what I had done before her. When I went to see her after she was settled at the convent I found it just the same as it was in the days when I was her age, many of the same sisters being there yet. It didn't seem as if a chair had been moved since I left: the same gong ringing each hour, the same little choir and organ— and I was still "Little Ethel" to the sisters. It was a very delightful experience.

During the third year of *Déclassée* Alf Hayman died, and I decided that next season I would like to join Arthur Hopkins, who had produced *The Jest* with Jack and Lionel, and who was interested, as I was, in starting a repertory company in New York.

I went to see Mr. Hopkins at his office and he asked me if I had ever read a play by Gerhart Hauptmann called *Rose Bernd*. I had not. He sent it to me and I read it. I thought it was magnificent, and when it was produced it made a profound impression.

It had been planned that the next play I was to do would be *As You Like It* and I had spent most of the summer and a good deal of time during the *Rose Bernd* run in studying Rosalind. But, for some reason, after my brother's great success in *Hamlet*, Mr. Hopkins thought it was more important to do *Romeo and Juliet*, which we had planned for the next season.

I found out after we were rehearsing it that Jane Cowl was going to do it and told Arthur Hopkins that I didn't want to do it, but he insisted on going on with it, partly because Robert Edmond Jones had already made sketches for the sets. His obstinacy was the immovable object tenfold and quite impossible to overcome. I made no impression whatever on him, but I should never have consented to do the play. It was sheer misery for me all the time we were doing it, and when it was over, I felt as if a great burden had been lifted from me.

This was not a successful venture. The public didn't like the scenery—they didn't like the company—they didn't like me. It had moments of great beauty and, curiously enough, although it was a real failure night after night, I got the most enormous return from the audience in the way of vibrant appreciation—that incommunicable something which passes between the player and the audience which no words can express. Many times I felt that they were saying to each other, "I don't know what the critics can mean. This is most beautiful. Why do they say it isn't good?"

A curious thing happened to me while I was playing Juliet. When I was lying on the tomb, supposedly dead, in the last act, the fact that I had to remain so still seemed to have a hypnotic influence on me and it was with the greatest difficulty and will power that I kept myself from literally becoming unconscious. One night I did for an instant lose consciousness.

Romeo and Juliet was a failure, but there were a lot of people who liked it. The principal one to me was Jack. This is what he wrote me about it:

Dearest Ethel:
I couldn't tell you half of what I really thought of your perform-ance, dear. It really, *really*, is great. It is *truly* magnificent, the finest thing you've ever done. I think I was wrong about the balcony scene not being passionate enough. It would make it too *objective* and the whole thing is just the other way.

Really Ethel, it is beautiful and you ought to be terribly proud
about it.

Much love,

Jake

The next piece we did was *The Laughing Lady*, so different in every way. It was the sort of play I had done before,
like *Lady Frederick* and *Cousin Kate*, and was much harder
for me to do than the big roles. A light comedy is the most
tiring of all to play, the most difficult to keep up. You are
taking the part of a person who is just like everyone in the
audience. And the fact that you have to be natural is much
harder than doing emotional parts. People don't realize this.
It is much more difficult to be convincing in a modern
comedy when every woman in the audience thinks she is
more or less like the woman you are playing.

After that tour, for a week I had the double delight of
playing with Uncle Jack in the Players' production of *The
School for Scandal*, which has always been one of my
favorite plays. I was Lady Teazle. She in a way is a laughing lady, too, but you have to approach her and play her
in an entirely different way. Artificiality of manner, speech
and gesture makes it easier to be good as Lady Teazle than
as *The Laughing Lady*. The very fact that one has a wig
on and is in a different costume helps to make it easier.

The production had a notable cast. Walter Hampden
played the part of a servant. So did Francis Wilson and
Grant Mitchell, while Robert Mantell did the small part of
Snake—exactly in the spirit of the repertory theater.
William Seymour directed us for the first few days and gave

Miss Barrymore in *The Kingdom of God,* which opened the
Ethel Barrymore Theatre in 1928 (Spencer Berger Collection)

Lionel, Ethel and John Barrymore in the motion picture *Rasputin and the Empress* (Spencer Berger Collection)

The world première of the film at the Astor Theatre, New York, December 23, 1932 (Spencer Berger Collection)

Ethel and John Barrymore with Diana Wynyard during the filming (Spencer Berger Collection)

Family gathering at the home of John Barrymore in Beverly Hills, summer, 1932. Left to right, Mr. and Mrs. Lionel Barrymore (Irene Fenwick) with John's son, Ethel Barrymore, Mrs. John Barrymore (Dolores Costello) with daughter, and Ethel Barrymore Colt. Standing, John Drew Colt, John Barrymore and Samuel Colt (Spencer Berger Collection)

Miss Barrymore in *The Corn Is Green* (Upper left, Vandamm photo, other photos by Bob Golby, Courtesy Spencer Berger Collection)

On Ethel Barrymore's 40th anniversary as a star she and Helen Hayes
talk by radio in New York to Lionel and John Barrymore in Hollywood
(Spencer Berger Collection)

With Cary Grant in the film *None but the Lonely Heart*, which won an Academy award. Note *Cousin Kate* picture in background (Spencer Berger Collection)

Ethel Barrymore in 1946 (Spencer Berger Collection)

Mrs. Eleanor Roosevelt presenting Miss Barrymore with the Barter Theatre Award, May 12, 1941 (Wide World)

Ethel Barrymore, Louis B. Mayer and Lionel Barrymore at Miss Barrymore's 70th birthday celebration, August 15, 1949 (Wide World)

Miss Barrymore with Ethel Colt Miglietta and John Drew Miglietta on the lawn at Mamaroneck (Photo by Toni Frissell, Courtesy of *Harper's Bazaar*)

us the traditional stage "business"—things he had in his old prompt books. We used Sheridan's original text, not Augustin Daly's version. The whole spirit was splendid, and it was a great pleasure to be in it. I did it as a labor of love and out of it came rich rewards.

After *Déclassée* had closed Jack had come to stay with me for a while at Mamaroneck. He was very unhappy and at a loose end, his wife having gone off to Europe. So I literally took him by the hand to French Lick, Indiana, with a little red Temple *Hamlet* in my pocket. At French Lick, Jack was bored, and I gave him the little red *Hamlet* and told him to learn one of the soliloquies and he did. When he read it to me, neither one of us was quite happy about it, but I still knew that the spark was there.

One day after he had come back to Mamaroneck with me, we went to lunch at the Carringtons' and a little later Jack asked me if Britt could take him over to see Margaret Carrington again. I said yes, and that was the last I saw of Jack until he emerged three months later. Margaret had a wonderful method of voice production and breath control which, added to Jack's native genius, gave him the supreme confidence that resulted in the *Hamlet* that the world will not forget.

Of course I saw him in it many times, but the most thrilling performance of all was a dress rehearsal just before the opening night. Jack didn't dress for it. He was just in his ordinary street clothes, and I suppose it was the greatest experience I ever had in a theater. He was superb, magnificent, unforgettable, and had in some mysterious way acquired that magical ease, as if he really were Hamlet. It was for me the fulfillment of all I had ever hoped for him and more.

While Jack was playing *Hamlet* the Moscow Art Theatre came to New York. They played Friday matinees and so I could go to see them and I was at their feet. You didn't need to know Russian to understand every word that was said. They were superb.

Jack and I used to take them to supper at a Russian restaurant run by a Czarist general who in those Prohibition days thoughtfully gave his compatriots vodka in small after-dinner coffee cups.

Madame Tchekovna was the only one of them who could speak English, and she kept telling us that they all wanted to see "the real Americans." It was some time before we understood that what they wanted to see was Harlem! It was no use trying to tell her that the real Americans were Red Indians, good and bad, and at last we did take them to a place in Harlem. The man who owned it was shot to death in front of it on the morning after we were there.

Jack gave a special matinee of *Hamlet* for them. He knew that something was wrong, and after the first act he sent for me and said, "What's the matter? What am I doing?"

I said, "You're pressing."

He said, "Yes, I guess I am."

Then he relaxed and was his usual great self again.

The Colony Club gave a dinner for the Russian company and asked Jack to make a speech, and he did—a very witty one. I remember his saying that the amazing thing about these people was that after playing together for so many years they still seemed to like each other.

Once while Jack was playing *Hamlet* I was playing in Washington and went to lunch with Mr. and Mrs. Coolidge at the White House. Mr. Coolidge had different food from us, just a sort of pap. There were several collie dogs sitting about and he would throw little bits of food to them. He said, "Saw your brother the other night in *Hamlet.* Very good. He made a speech between the acts, a very funny speech. Told some stories about his Negro valet, right in the middle of *Hamlet.* That's a good way to make speeches, funny stories. I know some funny stories, but I think the American public likes to think of their President as being a sort of solemn ass and I think I'll just go on being a solemn ass."

I came out of the White House laughing. Reporters were all over me wanting to know why. I said, "Just at something the President said," and they all fell flat on the grass.

Once when I was staying with Alec Woollcott on his island in Vermont, he drove me over to see the little town where Coolidge's father had a store and post office. I had a sudden terrific feeling about the night when the old gentleman answered the telephone and a voice asked him if the President of the United States was there.

"No, but the Vice President is."

"No," the voice said, "Mr. Harding has just died. Will you get the President to the phone?"

The old man called, "Cal."

"Have you got a Bible?" the voice said.

"Of course I've got a Bible."

"Then I guess you'd better swear him in."

And all at once the little town in the green Vermont hills was famous and telephone and telegraph lines were built up to that little country store. I always thought it made a marvelously American story. William Allen White wrote it beautifully.

Alec and I also went to see the little graveyard on the side of a hill where Coolidge is buried. His tombstone was small and simple just like his father's. The only thing about it that was different was the seal of the President of the United States.

After *The Laughing Lady,* my next play was *A Royal Fandango* by Zoë Akins. There was a young man in it who played a newspaper photographer, a very small part. He had one line to say, and I saw that he was very nervous, so I said to him, "Relax. That's all you have to do—just relax. It'll all be the same in a hundred years."

The young man's name was Spencer Tracy and he has been relaxing with notable success for twenty-five of those hundred years.

❧ VII ❧

Only Duse Has Moved
Me Like This

After another interlude of vaudeville in *The Twelve Pound Look* I had a sudden longing for England. Although I could stay for only a few days, I went over. I sent a note to Winston Churchill asking him to send me a ticket for the ladies' gallery at the House of Commons. He sent me one by his secretary, Sir Edward Marsh, and he and Winston and I had tea together in Winston's rooms.

Everything else in England—the place, the people, everything—seemed different. The only thing that didn't seem to have changed was the House of Commons. It interested me just as much as ever.

While I was there a man on a back bench stood up and made a wonderful speech about a very dull subject. It was Lloyd George, out of power, without responsibilities. He was so funny that all the Conservatives were laughing.

When I came back to New York, I could not find a new play that I liked, and Arthur Hopkins suggested a revival of *The Second Mrs. Tanqueray*, which was and is another of my favorite plays. I have always thought it was a great play apart from the fact that it was epoch-making—the first play written in English that can be called a problem play, the first one in which an English heroine had been a lady of the half world.

Although it had been originally produced more than thirty years earlier, it proved to be an extraordinary success, both in New York and on tour, and I played it all through the season. I remember how deeply Amy Lowell, a very hard person to please, was moved by it. She came back to my dressing room in Boston and said, "Only Duse has moved me like this."

I was thrilled by that. She was a wonderful person, Amy Lowell. Always when I played in Boston, I would go one day to lunch in Brookline at her house. There would always be other women there, but Miss Lowell never lunched with us because she worked all night. She would appear about three o'clock and talk to us about everything under the sun, smoking a large, very expensive cigar.

I think it was about this time that I went down to Washington for a big dinner party that the Edward McLeans were giving. I stayed at Mrs. J. Borden ("Daisy") Harriman's, and all kinds of people came in for tea—diplomats, Cabinet members, Senators, all talking with great solemnity about one thing: "Did you get a message from Mrs. McLean that we are to wear black ties?"

This was discussed in hushed, grave tones. It wasn't until we got to the McLeans' that we found out the reason for the message—Will Rogers was the guest of honor and he never wore a white tie!

Of course if anybody had worn a white tie, Will Rogers wouldn't have noticed it, and it always struck me as grimly humorous that such a triviality could have caused such excitement in one of the world's great capitals.

Afterward I came to know Evelyn McLean very well and often in Washington I would stay at Friendship with her and her two old great Danes and her ancient, rather decrepit watchman. She kept a fortune in jewels in a suitcase under her bed and she used to drag it out and put it on the bed and show me all the lovely things that had been her mother's. Even when she and little Evelyn went around the corner to the movies in tweed skirts and sweaters, she wore the Hope diamond. She never took it off till just before she went to sleep. Then she'd put it on the night table. I asked her what she'd do if someone broke in, and she opened a drawer of the table and there was a big revolver in it. She was very casual about it all.

Sometimes I would stay with a dear friend of hers and mine, that lovely, beguiling creature Cissie Patterson, in her beautiful house on Dupont Circle which she once lent to the Coolidges when the White House was being repaired. I had first known Cissie and her brother Joe—two people absolutely dripping with charm—in Chicago and later in New York. Cissie was running the Washington *Times Herald,* which she had first managed for Hearst and then bought from him.

There were other happy memories of those years. One of them is going to wonderful Sunday luncheons at the Swopes's at Great Neck. One of the first times I went there I heard Maggie, Herbert's wife, say casually to the maid they had had since they were married, "Mae, there'll be thirty-four for dinner."

There were, and one of them was Ring Lardner, who lived next door. Ring was one of my idols, wonderfully kind and charming. It was always thrilling to see him saunter onto the porch.

Just as I was writing this page a letter came from Herbert Swope. He had heard that I was writing this book and wrote to give me what he describes as his Word for Today about it.

Tell the truth, irregardless (as Jim Farley says) of what it may be. Truth is always more interesting.

And remember the two best rules of writing that were ever laid down:

The first, by the Red Queen in "Alice" when she was asked how Alice should tell a story: "That's very simple—begin at the beginning, go through to the end, then stop."

The second was by Lord Verulam, whom the peasants know as Francis Bacon: "Look into thine heart, then write."

I have tried my best to live up to all of these counsels.

Another of the happy memories is of going to Sunday night dinners with that magical Laurette Taylor and her husband, Hartley Manners, in their big house on Riverside Drive. She had made a silent picture of *Peg o' My Heart* and always after dinner they would show it to us. Some years afterward she said to me, "Ethel, did you ever see my picture *Peg o' My Heart*?"

I said, "All one winter."

I hadn't meant to be funny, but Laurette loved it and kept repeating it.

We were very fond of each other, and she would often say, "Here's Ethel, Hartley's favorite actress."

After *Mrs. Tanqueray* I played for a short season in *Hamlet* and *The Merchant of Venice* with Walter Hampden, whom I admire and love, both as a person and an actor.

Ophelia is my favorite Shakespearean part. She is often played by little flibbertigibbets chosen apparently for both their youth and imbecility, so that when Ophelia does go mad, the shock which Shakespeare meant the audience to feel is no shock at all. I think she is really a very subtle, tragic and beautifully poetic character.

Ophelia was Ellen Terry's favorite Shakespearean part, and I have always wished that I could have seen her in it.

The first part of Portia is very difficult, like algebra or a

EVENINGS AT EIGHT-FIFTEEN   MATINEES AT TWO-FIFTEEN

Beginning Saturday Evening, December 26th, 1925

WALTER HAMPDEN
and
ETHEL BARRYMORE
in SHAKESPEARE'S
THE MERCHANT OF VENICE

Entire scenic production designed and supervised by CLAUDE BRAGDON
Staged and directed by WALTER HAMPDEN

C A S T

THE DUKE OF VENICE	Philip Wood
THE PRINCE OF MOROCCO ⎫ *suitors to Portia* .	Ernest Rowan
THE PRINCE OF ARRAGON ⎭	Le Roi Operti
ANTONIO, *a merchant of Venice*	William Sauter
BASSANIO, *his friend, suitor to Portia* . . .	Maurice Colbourne

complicated fugue. It was a great comfort to come to the courtroom scene, which is at least straightforward, but I didn't like the idea of making the quality-of-mercy speech a speech. In the passage I say to Antonio, "Do you confess the bond?"

He says, "I do."

And I say, "Then must the Jew be merciful."

Shylock says, "On what compulsion must I, tell me that?"

And instead of making a speech I merely answered his question very quietly, "The quality of mercy is not strained," and then proceeded, still very quietly as the speech went on, becoming more and more legal and developing the plea that Portia was going to make.

It had a curious, overwhelming effect on the audience. I never heard such silence, and then a sort of gasp, much as to say, *"Why, that was the speech!"* Usually the audience is waiting for the speech and whispers it with Portia, especially the schoolchildren in the balcony at matinees. This time the audience was taken unawares, and the speech was almost over before they realized it was beginning. Even the schoolchildren were dumb with surprise when they realized it, which was a great comfort to me.

Again there wasn't any play that I wanted to do, and so I went back into vaudeville in *The Twelve Pound Look*, this time on a long tour during which I stayed in the same Kansas City hotel in which Sinclair Lewis lived while he was getting material for *Elmer Gantry*. On the way to my apartment I would have to pass the open door of his. It was always crowded with ministers of every denomination whom he was bullying, in the hope, I suppose, of extracting something for his book. He would stride around the room, pointing a finger at one of them after another and saying, "You know you don't believe in God."

They all seemed transfixed except one little Catholic priest who said, "Sit down, my son, and don't blaspheme."

That silenced Red for a moment. Then he said, "Will you have a drink, Father?"

"I will," said the priest.

Sometimes he would ask me in for a few minutes. That was where I met Burris Jenkins, a Protestant minister who had a radio audience of millions every Sunday. We became great friends, and I used to have dinner with him and Mrs. Jenkins. He asked me if I would come to hear him preach, and I said I wasn't supposed to do that but I would go to mass first and then come.

So he sent his son, who was about seventeen, to take me to mass and then bring me to the service at his church. It was very interesting, and, to me, utterly unlike church.

My next play was *The Constant Wife* by Somerset Maugham. We opened it in Cleveland, and on the first night my old sick agony of terror caught up with me at last. The devastating thing about it was that, although my mind was blank, I still knew what was happening. Even with George Cukor, the stage manager, hiding in the fireplace with the manuscript trying to prompt me, I couldn't remember some of my lines. The next day the Cleveland papers intimated that I didn't know them and suggested that a city as large and important as Cleveland deserved better treatment. But the point was that I did know my lines. I was letter perfect in them the following night, and I had been letter perfect at dress rehearsal. This one night was the only time that the old terror ever really overcame me.

When Maugham came backstage after the play, looking rather grim, I said, "I ruined your play tonight but never mind. It's going to run two years."

And it did and more.

But Maugham was leaving the next day on his way to Japan and never saw it again.

Aubrey Smith played with me in *The Constant Wife*. One night in New York he came to my dressing room and

The Constant Infidelities

Miss Barrymore Returns Handsomely in a Clever Comedy of Extra-Maritals.

By GILBERT W. GABRIEL.

Marriage came in for some artful mocking at the Maxine Elliott Theater last night; and Ethel Barrymore came in for a cheering welcome. It was Maugham's newest, "The Constant Wife," a comedy of several sorts of felicities, graces, satisfactions. Those who prefer their truths smartly put will regard it as among the most enjoyable sessions the current stage plays host to.

This, by all counts, seems to be Somerset Maugham's first play hereabout since his "The Camel's Back" failed to live up to its smiles. For Miss Barrymore it is a number of celebrative things: A return to Maugham after almost a score of years.

'THE CONSTANT WIFE.'

Comedy in three acts, by W. Somerset Maugham, presented by the Charles Frohman Company in the Maxine Elliott Theater. Starring Ethel Barrymore, Mrs. Culver............Muriel Terry, Lewis Beulter..............Thomas A. Shipley, Martha Culver.............C. Haddon Chambers.

(New York Sun, November 30, 1926)

asked me, "How long do you think the play is going to run?"

I said, "Forever, apparently. Why, Aubrey?"

"Because," he said, "I should really go home to see my dad."

I thought he himself was quite an old man. It required a lot of self-control to keep from laughing. He did go and we had to replace him for a while. I nearly died without him.

He was a great cricketer, and when he was at Cambridge had played for England. When he was over eighty, he organized a cricket team among the English actors in Hollywood and played on it himself, appearing in striped blazer and flannels. He was a very much loved man.

The three years that I played in *The Constant Wife* were three of the ugliest years of the twenties, but the whole period was a period of ugliness, of ugly fashions, ugly manners, even ugly dances like the Charleston, and ugliest of all to me was the self-pity of the young "intellectuals" who were happy about being so sorry for themselves, so proud of being what they loved to call "the lost generation."

I was spared a lot of that ugliness because I was so busy playing in *The Constant Wife* through those three years that I did not have time to see much of the lost generation, but what I saw of them I didn't like. And how glad I am that I never saw my England in the hands of the "bright young people" who were the lost generation over there.

Of course it wasn't the generation that was lost but only a handful of unpleasant people, completely unlike the millions of sane, decent young men and women who had no time to be sorry for themselves because they were too busy at working and playing and living.

It was one of those people who for a while lifted all of us, even the young, melancholy intellectuals themselves, above the muddy sentimentality and defeatism of the age— a young man named Charles Lindbergh.

I shall always remember what I saw and heard in Times

Square on that afternoon when the news bulletins announced his safe arrival in Paris—the thousands of voices blending into one exultant cry, the shining brightness of self-forgetting triumph that was in every face. Most vividly I remember seeing it in the faces of two taxi drivers getting out of their cabs to throw their arms around each other.

I like to remember, too, one evening at Town Hall when a little colored girl named Florence Mills, wearing a short white dress, came out on the stage alone to sing a concert. She sang so beautifully; it was a great and thrilling experience.

Toward the end of the long, long run of *The Constant Wife* Zoë Akins, who was working for the Shuberts, came to me and told me that they wanted to build a theater and name it after me. They also had a play that I loved, *The Kingdom of God*. So I went over to their management, they built the Ethel Barrymore Theatre and I opened it with *The Kingdom of God*.

Percy Hammond wrote a nice thing about that theater. He said he was perfectly sure that Miss Barrymore would rather have it called the John Drew Theatre and he was so right!

I had known Percy and Florence Hammond when he was drama critic for the Chicago *Tribune*. I have always made a point of not knowing dramatic critics—I never really knew or liked Alec Woollcott until after he had stopped being one—but I always loved Percy Hammond. He was a graceful, exquisite writer; the only American critic, I think, who wrote about the theater beautifully. Henry Mencken is the only other critic whom I would put way up, a mischievous oddity and brilliant, whom it was always a pleasure for me to see in Baltimore.

Percy should never have moved from Chicago to New York, where he was never happy. He and Florence had a little house at East Hampton, and once when I was staying with Uncle Jack, I went to see them. It wasn't far so I walked. A big colored woman opened the door and said: "No, they out."

I said, "Well, I'd like to leave a message for them. Will you tell them that Miss Barrymore—"

She interrupted with a beautifully dismissing wave of her hand, said, "Oh, I never could remember that," and shut the door in my face. I could hear her laughing all the way back to her kitchen.

In *The Kingdom of God* I was a nun. In the first act I was a novice in a convent that took care of old men. In the second, I was twenty-nine, in a convent where bad girls came to have their babies, and in the last act I was seventy-two, the mother superior of an orphanage. I loved the play and so did everybody else. Then I did a worldly play called *The Love Duel* and alternated them on tour for eighty weeks. That was a wonderful experience because the two plays were so different. Louis Calhern played opposite me in *The Love Duel* and gave a magnificent performance.

In *The Kingdom of God* I began to direct my plays. I used my own name, E. M. Blyth, because I wanted a break, and I got it. There was praise for the direction from many sources.

On the first night of *The Kingdom of God* in Chicago,

when I went down the alleyway to the Harris Theatre, I saw a lot of men and couldn't imagine what they were doing there. When I asked, I was told that they were detectives in plain clothes who were surrounding the theater because there were going to be two gangs out in front.

There was a stagehand who I always insisted was in with the gangsters. I looked through a hole in the curtain and said to him, "I see your friend Al Brown in front."

"What do you mean?" he said.

I said, "Isn't that he?"

"Yes," he said, "but how did you know his name was Al Brown?"

I said, "I've heard that Al Capone calls himself Al Brown now and then."

As always I could see everything that went on in the audience, and all through the play I could see Capone sitting there, holding his wife's hand, with the tears pouring down his face.

Other actors were threatened in Chicago to make them contribute to alleged charities, and some of them were beaten when they didn't pay, but I was never threatened. Word had evidently gone out to leave me alone.

When we played in Los Angeles, I stayed with Jack in Beverly Hills. I remember his coming down to see the first night and driving me back afterward. All the way he was very quiet. He didn't say much except the usual things about loving it all. When we got home, his household was in bed—he was a bachelor at the moment, thank God! I always have coffee after a performance, and we went to the

kitchen to make it. When he had the coffee-making thing
working, he suddenly turned to me and said very abruptly,
"Why don't they cough?"

I said, "Oh, you mustn't let them cough."

"What the hell do you mean?" he said. "They coughed
in *Hamlet*."

I thought that was so endearing! I said again, "You
mustn't let them cough."

"What do you mean? You can't stop them from
coughing."

"Yes, you can."

"How?"

"I don't know. You turn on number eight or number ten
or whatever it is, and they just don't cough."

I have always been able to do something that keeps the
audience from coughing. I don't know what it is. I don't
think the voice has anything to do with it, but maybe it
has. You don't look at the cougher. You just know that they
must not cough. That's all.

That is one of the reasons why, after a play, you find that
the thing you must do to an audience has made you very
tired. You've fought ten rounds and you do it six nights
a week and two matinees. I was always enormously conscious of the audience. If they seem slightly hostile, the job
is to win them over and it is an extracurricular job. At the
end of such a day you just gradually let down the tension.
No sleep right away, not for me certainly. If there was
somebody to talk to, fine. If not, I would read into the night.
I mean well into the morning.

That time when we played *The Kingdom of God* in Los

Angeles was one of the few times I really saw Jack after the tour in *Sunday*. I stayed with him for two weeks. He was working all day on a movie, and I had to leave for the theater about the time he came home. I didn't like to keep him up waiting for me, but I did see him some days when he wasn't working at the studio.

Working in films is a lazy man's existence compared to working in the theater where, if you're a star, there is a terrific responsibility. You have to be always on top. You can't let down for a moment, or everybody else lets down without knowing that he is doing it.

As a matter of fact, it is rare that a performance is missed because of the illness of a player. Women on the stage have to do a great deal of traveling but can never have a cold or a headache; you are carried onto the train with a temperature, and that night you play Missoula. Actresses are supposed to rise above all the natural ills of the human body, and, by George, they do!

That's the truth behind that ridiculous, noble-sounding phrase, "The show must go on." The reason the show must go on is because a lot of people will be hungry if it doesn't, because the theater will close and salaries stop.

There is another phrase which I have always thought just as ridiculous—to say, of playing a role: "I *was* that person. I lost myself in the part." You'd lose everybody. How would you give some poor wretched actor a cue? The curtain would have to come down and the other actors, who were not lost, would have every right to overpowering indignation.

With some people acting is an instinctive thing and they

get by with it. Sometimes it's good. But the happy medium is a combination of the instinct and the mind.

Perhaps this is the place to add that often when I go to the theater I remember the lovely, lovely, old-fashioned footlights and think, "Oh, God, give 'em back!" The man who started modern lighting was Gordon Craig, Ellen Terry's son. Some of his ideas were magnificent, but those who followed in his footsteps sometimes got so carried away with their imaginative brilliance that they were much more interested in lighting a turret or a flight of steps than an actor's face, which I have always felt was more important— or at least equal. Of course both things have occasionally been accomplished by a genius who is luckily as much interested in the emotional play of an actor's face as in the beauties of a stone wall or a bit of Venetian brocade.

When *The Kingdom of God* closed, I went to Paris to meet Sister, who had been at school in Verona. We went to London, where the boys joined us when their school term was over. The hotels were so crowded that Sister and I had to stay in one and the boys in another. The expense of it was using up all the money we had for the summer until I met Bobby Newton at a party and he said he had a little house that we could have for five pounds a week. It was off Kings Road in Bywater Street, a tiny little house that just fitted us. It was perfectly charming and we made it our London headquarters when we wanted to go to a theater.

Anna Peterson—she said there were too many Petersons in Norway and changed her name to Patterson, but we always called her the Scandinavian Nightingale—had been my maid ever since Berthe had left me, twenty years before. She had cut short her holiday in Norway to come to England and look for a house in the country for us. She found a very nice one in Surrey, quite a big one, with a tennis court, and we spent the summer there. Russell came to England and would come down to dinner once a week and occasionally we would dine with him in London and go to a play.

Once when we were in London, I took Sammy and Jackie to lunch with the Winston Churchills. I remember how wonderful Winston was to them and how thrilled they were. And I remember taking Sister to that year's theatrical garden party—a wonderful opportunity for me to see, all together, many people I hadn't seen for years. All the stars had booths. I remember Gladys Cooper sitting at a small one, selling her own photographs and looking perfectly beautiful, and Tallulah Bankhead, running the treasure hunt and rushing over to take full charge of us. She asked us to wait till she was through at the booth and then come to her house and dine. So after we had seen Gerald du Maurier and all the other people I knew, we drove in Tallulah's beautiful Bentley to her charming flat in Farm Street, Berkeley Square, and dined there. She couldn't have been kinder or nicer to us all. It was truly a wondrous day.

I took the three children to lunch with Gerald and Muriel du Maurier at Hampstead. The boys played tennis with Gerald's daughters, Daphne and Jean, and Gerald was so funny about their manners. He said, "Are all American children so well mannered?"

I said I hadn't noticed anything different about their manners.

We spent a Sunday, too, at Walton with Anthony and Betty Hope and their children. I remember Anthony's taking me into his library and showing me a long line of his books and saying, with his funny little giggle, "A modest contribution."

He was the same sweet, wonderful person he had always been.

The summer was a heavenly one for all of us. I was relaxed because I had settled on my play for the next season. It was *Scarlet Sister Mary*. I had the manuscript with me and would occasionally look it over, studying it, and Sister would read it, too.

One night in our stateroom on the *Berengaria*, coming back to New York, when I thought Sister was asleep, she suddenly said, "Mother, I don't want to come out."

I said, "Why not?"

"I want to go on the stage. I want to play Seraphine in *Scarlet Sister Mary*."

"Are you sure?" I said. I wasn't prepared for this at all. I had never thought she wanted to go on the stage, and everything had been arranged for her debut—orchestra, room at the Colony Club, everything.

She said, "Oh, yes, I'm sure. I've thought about it a lot."

She did play the part and she was perfectly lovely in it. My cousin, Georgie Mendum, was in it, too, and we played it all through that season in New York and on tour.

It was lovely having Sister in the company with me. There was a very special kind of happiness in seeing her so charming, so sure in her part. When she first came on the stage, smiling, it always seemed to radiate a glow to every corner of the theater.

Although I had loved *Scarlet Sister Mary,* I thought it would be a wonderful contrast next fall to go back to the white powdered wigs of *A School for Scandal,* which also had a long run in New York and on tour.

The Winston Churchills came over to New York that winter, and one afternoon, when Winston was walking up Park Avenue from the Waldorf on his way to Bernard Baruch's, he was hit by a taxicab and rather seriously injured. Before he lost consciousness he told the police that it was not the taxi driver's fault but his, that he had been thinking of something else and hadn't realized that he wasn't in England where cars would have been coming from the other side.

In the hospital, as soon as he had recovered from the first shock, he began to write an article entitled "My New York Misadventure" which he sold to a syndicate for $2,500! I went to see him as soon as he came back from the hospital to the Waldorf and he said, "You know, Ethel, I have a terrible past."

I think he was thinking about the time he left the Conservative party and for a few years was a Liberal. He was always chiding himself like that, more or less humorously.

At the end of the regular season I was asked to play *A School for Scandal* in summer stock, bringing only a few members of the company. I said I would accept only on condition that my whole company came with me. On these terms we played through the whole summer season of sixteen weeks.

In the fall there was again no play that I wanted to do

and again I went back into vaudeville with *The Twelve Pound Look* until the following spring, when Metro-Gold-wyn-Mayer, who had decided to make a picture called *Rasputin and the Empress* wanted Lionel and Jack and me to act in it together and I was delighted with the idea.

When I came out they told me to leave the train at Pasadena to avoid the photographers and the newsmen, which I did. And of course all the photographers and newsmen were there. And so was Jack, whom I hadn't seen for two or three years.

He put his cheek against mine and embraced me and I was sure all the reporters and photographers thought he was telling me how wonderful it was to see me again but what he was really muttering into my hair was "For God's sake, get Bill Daniels."

I knew I would learn, later, the meaning of this remark and I waited till the photographers had finished and we were in the car. Then I said: "Who is Bill Daniels?"

"He's a cameraman," Jack said, "the best one in the world. He takes all those sweetbreads away from under my eyes. Garbo won't make a picture without him."

I said, "But, Jack, I wouldn't even know how to go about getting him."

He said, "You're new out here. You ask for him and you'll get him."

So I did ask Irving Thalberg for him and we did get him.

Making *Rasputin* with Lionel and Jack was one of the very few times all three of us were together after our early childhood days, but I hardly saw them except at the studio. When you're making a picture, you don't have time to see people and I was in Hollywood only for that picture.

It was great fun to be with them, of course, and I saw them at the studio as often as I could, which unfortunately wasn't too often, as there wasn't much time for anything except work, especially as the script was written day by day on the set, sometimes on the backs of old envelopes. Often I would learn a scene and then find that I would have to learn an entirely new one after I was on the set.

I had always been terrified of microphones and I was more terrified than ever when Lionel said to me, "The first thing to remember is that the microphone is right here," and he held his hand over his head—not very far over it.

When you speak in the theater, you know they have to hear you in the back row of the gallery. You speak very quietly but you make them hear you. It is a very different technique from that of the movie microphone, as different as violin and piano.

And, incidentally, I have always felt that one of the most important things about acting is listening. Sometimes it is more important than speaking.

Of course there was no truth in the nonsensical publicity stories about quarrels between us that were put out while we were making the picture. We were all actors, working at a job, and besides, we didn't know each other well enough to quarrel. You must remember that we were always very frighteningly polite to each other. Scene stealing between Lionel and Jack was just a joke. They did it for fun. The only thing I quarreled with was some parts of the story which I didn't think should be done. After I left they were done, and the company was sued because of them and had to pay heavy damages.

The children had come out with me. My agent had rented a house for us in Beverly Hills, an enormous one complete with tennis courts and swimming pool which I hardly ever saw, although I would hear the children's voices coming from them when I came home dead tired from the studio.

The Olympic Games were held in Los Angeles while we were making *Rasputin* and I managed to get to the opening day and see the March of Nations. It was all very impressive, but the most impressive thing about it, I regret to say, was the Italians. They were all in black. They moved as one person and as they passed the presidential box and gave the Fascist salute, it was as if one arm went up. It was a terrific sight, and curiously enough, not ominous.

That was the only day on which I could go to the games because I had to be at the studio, but Russell came out and took the children every day and came to dinner every night.

I remember going to the "première" of a picture, the first one I had ever seen. This one in the middle of the depression was very different from those that I had heard and read about when the bystanders applauded the people who drove by them in big cars. This time there was no applause. The onlookers on the sidewalks were silent and sullen as people wearing furs and jewels rode by them in the big cars. It was a very uncomfortable experience.

After *Rasputin* I came back to New York to do *Encore*, soon renamed *An Amazing Career* by Arthur Hopkins. It was a very amusing play about an opera singer who gets progressively younger as the play goes on and marries and marries and marries. When she is about to marry for the last time, she appears in a white organdie dress with a blue sash. It was a very funny play, but there was nothing funny about the depression in which we were doing it, the bad days when there wasn't any money except scrip, which was only good where it was issued. Finally, when we were in Chicago, and the Government ordered all the banks to close, there wasn't any money at all, and although the play had been doing very well indeed, we had to close it.

That next year was a very bad and harrowing time, the only year after I first went on the stage when I was not at work. I did some summer stock in *The Constant Wife* but otherwise we stayed at Mamaroneck and had a very thin time.

Late in the winter, when I went to London and played *The Twelve Pound Look* at the Palladium for a week, an astounding thing happened. They didn't like the play! They hated it! They said it was old-fashioned—I don't know what they didn't say about it. I had banked on it for so many years, had thought it was practically a classic, and it was a shock to discover that as far as England was concerned its day was past.

I motored down to see the Churchills at Chartwell and spent the night. Winston showed me about the place. I remember him waving his hand at the grounds and the house and saying: "Ethel, all this out of my pen!"

He was out of power then, a voice crying unheeded in the wilderness against the feeble temporizings of Ramsay Mac-Donald, and prophesying with what was proved to be uncanny accuracy the consequence of giving way before Hitler's increasing belligerency, which Ramsay MacDonald and Chamberlain after him fondly imagined could be turned aside with soft answers.

Dangerous as I saw they were, both Hitler and Mussolini seemed to me even more ridiculous, and I always thought that laughter could have been a most effective weapon against them both. All during the time when their power was growing, I longed for Peter Dunne and Mr. Dooley.

I thought Ramsay MacDonald was a confused man; a kind of British Henry Wallace as it seems to me now. I suppose there is no "gooder" man than Henry Wallace. He has the very highest ideals but just doesn't know the score. Like Ramsay MacDonald, he seems to be a very tragic figure.

I came back to Mamaroneck for the summer and in the autumn I played in *L'Aiglon* with Eva Le Gallienne. Sister had the part of Fanny Elssler, the dancer, and although she was over nineteen, she went through the painful process of taking ballet lessons in order to make her entrance on the points of her toes. It was beautifully done, but nobody ever noticed. They just took it for granted that she could walk on her toes. That always gave me a pain around my heart. There were so many times in my life when there have been pains around my heart! In fact when I began to write this book, every now and then I thought of calling it *So Many Tears,* but I decided that this would be rather a melancholy title and also I had managed through the years to dam up the tears.

I never realized then that Sister was to become something new in our family—a wonderful singer. She was the only private pupil Maggie Teyte ever took in America, and she has gone on to a long and successful career of most beautiful singing in concert and opera. Her voice has extraordinary range and she uses it with magnificent artistry. And she has been equally successful in her private career of marriage and motherhood.

Both of my sons, too, have helped to make me happy. Jackie has been happily married for fourteen years to Marjorie Dow, of Boston, and they live in the Mamaroneck house. And I don't know how I could manage without Sammy, who adds so much to my comfort, living out here with me and looking after my affairs.

After *L'Aiglon* I couldn't find a play I wanted to do and, except for twenty-six weeks when I did a radio series, there were some lean times. I enjoyed working in radio. A manuscript is such a lovely thing to lean against. Later I was to find that I liked working in television, too. They are learning to do so many interesting things with it. But there were some good times, too, in those summers when I went to stay with Eleo at Prides' Crossing and with that lovely, glowing creature, Katharine Cornell, at Martha's Vineyard, and at Sands Point with Herbert and Margaret Swope. I still go to see Herbert and Margaret if they are at Sands Point when I am in the East; our friendship has gone on through all the years and I am utterly devoted to them both.

The plays I have most enjoyed doing are *Déclassée*, *The Second Mrs. Tanqueray*, *The Constant Wife* and *The Corn*

Is Green. Such plays seldom come along. After the lean times I played briefly for the Theatre Guild in *The Ghost of Yankee Doodle* by Sidney Howard.

During that engagement I read in a newspaper that Lionel, who had been making a movie in England, was in New York on his way to Hollywood. I called him up and asked, politely as always, if I could come to see him.

He said, just as politely, "No, I'll come to see you."

When he came, he told me about having seen *Whiteoaks* in London. He said that it was an amusing play with an amusing part in it for me and I ought to get hold of it. That same evening an English producer named Payne-Jennings called up and said, "I've got the rights of a play called *Whiteoaks*. Do you mind playing a woman of 102?"

I said, "I'd be perfectly delighted. That's just what I feel."

So I played a woman of 102 all that season in New York, for part of the summer in stock and all the next season on tour.

During that tour I often hired a car to take me from one city to the next instead of going by train. It was good to see the country and to breathe clean air. In Montana I remember driving between pines as high on one side as I could see and stretching far below me on the other and between them the road covered with frozen snow and nothing else, just the pine trees and the road. A tire went and when we stopped to change it, I said to the driver, "I'd better get out and walk up and down to keep warm."

I did. I looked up and looked down. It was like being alone in the world, and then, suddenly, I saw a very small sign, so small that I could hardly see it. It said: CONTINENTAL

DIVIDE. I will never forget those black pines and that white snow, the most beautiful sight I ever saw!

There is another day that remains in my memory, when I was to play a summer stock engagement in Maine. I had been playing in Boston and had my own car and Britt, my chauffeur. We left Boston early Sunday morning, driving through Massachusetts, Vermont and New Hampshire on the way to Bangor. The extraordinary thing was that, without seeing a signpost, without anyone telling us what state we were in, we knew. The Green Mountains of Vermont, the White Mountains of New Hampshire and the Maine landscape all were unmistakable.

Again the shadows were deepening over the world, and this time they were too visible to be ignored or misunderstood. I had been living under them so long that there was no shock of disbelieving amazement when, early one September morning, without knowing why I did it, I reached out to turn on my radio and heard the tired, tragic voice of Chamberlain announcing that England was again at war. Again, as it had been for me in the first war, work was a blessed necessity. In *Farm of Three Echoes,* a play about Boer people in South Africa, I played a woman of ninety-seven, and I loved doing it. We opened in Princeton and played Washington and Baltimore before coming to New York, and a member of the psychiatric department at Johns Hopkins wrote me that my performance was "the most magnificent portrayal of senility" they had ever seen. I was slightly startled but delighted.

In the spring I played in *An International Incident* by

Vincent Sheean. Guthrie McClintic produced and directed
it and he was fun to work with, but it was a light play, quite
different from the serious one that the title and the author's
name and the state of the world led people to expect, and it
had only a short run.

I found some solace for the downfall of France in the
splendor of spirit with which the people of England turned
that terrible defeat into the triumph of Dunkirk, and in their
turning, at last, to the leader whose vision had never been
deceived, whose courage never faltered. I think I knew, even
when it was hard to hope and impossible to believe, that my
dear friend Winston Churchill's promise of blood and sweat
and toil and tears was an even surer promise of victory.

Herman Shumlin had secured the American rights of
The Corn Is Green, and asked me to read it. When he came
to the Colony Club to talk to me about it, I said, "You can't
be Stanislavskyish about this. It's a simple play about a
simple Englishwoman with the gift of teaching, who gets a
wonderful chance."

He looked a little startled that anybody should have an
opinion about anything, but he controlled his apparent
amazement and we came quickly to an agreement.

I was very much astonished at the first rehearsal, when
all the company were sitting around reading their parts from
the manuscript, to see Miss Lillian Hellman also sitting
there. I don't know whose grave was whirling more rapidly,
my grandmother's or Mr. Frohman's, but I suddenly realized
that a new day and a new way had come upon the theater.

Miss Ethel Barrymore Unabashed By 40 Years

By Nathaniel Benchley

DID you ever collar President Roosevelt and say: "What do you think about politics?" Well, that's nothing. I saw Ethel Barrymore and asked her to tell me something of herself and the theater.

The reason I think I had the tougher assignment is that Miss Barrymore is now in her tenth term as a star, and next Tuesday will celebrate the fortieth anniversary of her opening in "Captain Jinks of the Horse Marines." Also, in another couple of years she will have been on the stage for half a century, and over a stretch like that you run into many more experiences than just sitting around an old office for eight years.

Fortieth anniversary of the opening of *Captain Jinks* was celebrated during the run of *The Corn Is Green*. (*New York Herald Tribune*, February 2, 1941)

The play and I were instant and terrific successes and believe me it was high time for that success. It came at a crucial moment in my life and made all the difference.

Perhaps out of that success I drew the strength of spirit I needed to bear, for the second time, the sudden nearness of a war that had seemed far away. For me this war came very near, for Sammy enlisted immediately after Pearl Harbor and before long Jackie too was in uniform. There is no comfort for a woman whose sons have gone to war, but the next best thing is to have, as I had it through those heavy years, the blessing of hard work.

The Corn Is Green, after fourteen months in New York, ran for two years more on tour, a tour in which, after having played every city in the country, we went straight back and played exactly the same cities over again.

During the tour Mr. Piazzi of RKO got on the train at Portland, Oregon, and asked me to read the script of a moving picture, *None but the Lonely Heart,* on my way to San Francisco. I read it that night, and in the morning when Mr. Piazzi came to my stateroom and asked me how I liked it, I said I liked it very much but it would be impossible for me to do it, as I had to finish the tour.

He said, "We know all about that. All we want to know now is, do you like the part well enough to play it? If you do we will make the necessary arrangements with Mr. Shumlin."

I said, "That will be very nice," and dismissed the matter from my mind as a fantasy. But while we played San Francisco and Los Angeles, the necessary arrangements *were* made, and they were fantastic.

RKO agreed to pay all the company's salaries during the time I was making the picture, to reimburse Mr. Shumlin for all the receipts that would have been taken in, during that time, by the theaters where the play had been booked, and to reimburse the theaters for all cancellations and for the money they would have made!

I liked the picture and I liked Clifford Odets who directed

it and David Hempstead who produced it and Cary Grant who was my son. And of course it was very pleasant later to get the Oscar. The very last day I worked was when I died in the prison. The make-up man walked over to my dressing room with me when it was over and he said, "I feel very silly. I had the menthol stuff all ready to make you cry and when I saw tears gushing out of your eyes and pouring down your cheeks, I really did feel pretty silly."

I finished the picture at noon and I was on the train to go back to *The Corn Is Green* at one o'clock.

One of the things that I seem to remember clearly about that long, long tour in *The Corn Is Green* is the little boys—infants—in uniform, saying good-by to their mothers and their girls at railroad stations. And the stars in the windows of the little shacks beside the track—there were four gold stars in the window of one house that you couldn't believe had more than one room in it. The first war had been different; then it was bands marching along Fifth Avenue, cheers and doughnuts.

More clearly I remember an afternoon at the Colonial Theatre in Boston. I was waiting in my dressing room after a matinee—I often used to have food brought to me in the theater between a matinee and the evening performance instead of going out to dinner—when they brought me word from the box office that Lionel was calling me from California.

I knew it must be something very important. As I ran back of the boxes toward the front of the house, I fell and broke a bone in my ankle and I didn't know it until after I had got to the box office, and Lionel had told me that Jack was dead.

When I started back, I couldn't walk. I had the ankle strapped up and managed to get through the play that evening, but I had to spend the next two nights in a hospital.

Although I saw very little of Jack during our lives, I still miss him every day, as I did when I wrote to Alec Woollcott:

I am feeling—as I am sure you know—laid low. So many memories of my little brother, so long ago, when we were all so young and knew and expected so little, and it didn't matter.

After *The Corn Is Green* when I was playing in *Embezzled Heaven*, based on Franz Werfel's novel, I got pneumonia and almost died. Perhaps I ought to have died, when everybody was saying such nice things about me. There was one editorial in the *New York Times* that was so wonderful I simply had to know who wrote it. So I asked Herbert Swope to find out for me and he said, "I'm glad to know you read it. I was going to send it to you." And he did find out that it was Brooks Atkinson who wrote the editorial. It was Brooks Atkinson, too, who said about my performance in *The Corn Is Green,* "Let's stop quibbling and just call it a masterpiece!"

After I was well somebody told me that one night those electric signs that scamper around the Times building had said, all in one breath:

GENERAL MAC ARTHUR LANDS AT LEYTE ETHEL BARRYMORE'S
TEMPERATURE LOWER

When I was well enough to travel, the doctor sent me

down to Hot Springs, where it snowed all the time I was there.

To her great happiness—and mine—Sister had become engaged to Romeo Miglietta, a charming Italian, an engineer, who had spent most of his life in England and America. He was able to leave his work for a short time just after I went to Hot Springs and Sister thought it would be wonderful to be married then and spend their honeymoon at Hot Springs while I was there. And so to my happy thankfulness they did.

That pneumonia was the second of the only two important illnesses I have had in my long life in the theater, a life which makes demands on physical strength that kill many, many people very young.

My next play was Philip Barry's *The Joyous Season*, in which again I had the part of a nun. I did not bring it to New York. I loved it and did not want it to be buffeted, so I closed it at the end of the run in Chicago.

I had had pneumonia; I was suddenly getting lots of colds; I decided it might be better for me to pursue the sun of southern California, so out I came and began to make motion pictures. Then I decided to make California my home and keep on making pictures. It wasn't as strenuous as the theater. I had given fifty years to the theater and felt that I had done my bit, and besides, lately, in the theater in New York, I had come to feel a little as if I were Ruth amid the alien corn. And, incidentally, in all the years I have never ceased to miss Mr. Frohman.

❧ VIII ❧

Thank You, Mr. President

When I first came to California to live I had a tiny little house on Laurel Canyon Drive, perched on a hill—just a one-person house. There was no room even for a maid. Then Sammy joined me and I began looking for a larger place.

Zoë Akins said one day, "Have you ever been to Palos Verdes?"

I said, "I never even heard of it."

We drove out there and, all of a sudden, it was entirely different from any other place in southern California where I had been. A place of magical beauty. Ahead of us on the road I saw a house with a high brick wall entirely covered with a blaze of climbing geraniums—pale mauve, pale pink, coral, white. They seemed to be every color and the next color you saw was the blue, blue sea. A big man was standing at the gate.

"Do you mind if we stop a minute just to admire the flowers?" I asked.

He said, "No. Have you come to look at the house?"

It was for rent! We went in and I took it.

The house was surrounded by trees, with one huge willow, and beautiful flowers, a perfectly lovely place. From my bedroom upstairs there was a big, wide balcony. I used to sit out there, looking across the whole Pacific Ocean—at China. (Of course, what I was really looking at on days when it wasn't hazy was Catalina.)

When guests from England and other foreigners came they couldn't understand why anyone lived anywhere else.

Lionel came to lunch one day, took one look at the house and said, "Well, Mrs. Doheny—!"

It was not a palazzo, but it did have a beautiful view. Elsie de Wolfe said it was too far out for her to come to lunch, but her husband, Sir Charles Mendl, came and told me the place was beautiful. Finally Elsie heard so much about it that she decided to see it for herself. So she came and I said, "Charles says this place is like the South of France."

Elsie said, "Not at all!—Capri."

The house was not too far out for me but everyone else thought it was, and so we finally left it after four years for Pacific Palisades.

In California I soon found that you see so many nice people with widely differing interests. Aldous Huxley, Thomas Mann, Artur Rubinstein and Horowitz live here because they find it restful and like the outdoor life. Bob Hutchins, a great friend of mine, is here now, too, and Christopher Isherwood and Gerald Heard. Friends from all parts of the world keep arriving, stopping on their way here and there. It is always pleasant to hear from Walter Hampden when he comes out to do a picture. The last two times he brought Mabs, his wife, with him and she's sweet, too.

Then there are the old friends: George Cukor who, of all the people who have achieved great success and wealth in Hollywood, is unchanged, he is just the same person he was when he was getting $50 a week, just as kind, just as amusing and just as good a friend of mine; there is Charlie Brackett, too, whom I had known for years in New York, and Elizabeth, his wife, a great person; Mildred and Edwin

Knopf, two fine people; and it is always pleasant when Katharine Hepburn is here.

New friends, too. I was in a west side market, ordering things for the house and suddenly saw a man sauntering along, eating an apple.

He said, "Hello, Miss Barrymore."

"Hello, Mr. Crosby," I said.

We sort of grinned at each other and he waved the hand holding the apple. "My lunch."

That was the way we met and that was the end of the conversation. My children and I had been mad about Bing Crosby from the days of his earliest records and we had them all. "In a Five and Ten Cent Store" and all the rest.

When I met his wife, Dixie, for the first time I was enchanted by her. It was only a few months before her illness. She gave a surprise birthday party for Bing and it really was a surprise. He is probably the only person in Hollywood for whom you could have a surprise party. He had been at the studio all day, and came home and found 250 people at the house.

Dixie looked so pretty, so young and attractive. At first I thought she was blonde and then, when I saw her under the lights of the dance floor, I realized that her hair was silver.

When I played in a picture with Bing it was one of the most charming experiences I have had in the movies. He is so relaxed, so nice, just being around him is heaven.

Hollywood is a fairly make-believe place with distinct sets of people. Whether these sets are influenced by money or by snobbery, who knows? But there they are. I don't

think it's true to say that, because of Hollywood, people with
real talent have been lost to the theater. Nobody is lost to the
theater unless they want to be. And if they want to be lost,
let them.

There are as many different kinds of people in Hollywood
as there are in other parts of the world. And that is diverting.
Even the extremes are diverting.

For example, there was the woman of, shall we say, very
small beginnings (there is nothing at all wrong with small
beginnings) who went to a luncheon. Afterward, describing
the dining-room table, she raised her hands in horror. "My
dear, they had commercial silver!"

Once my brother Jack stopped one of the magnates who
was screaming at him and shaking a finger in his face. Jack
said, "Put that finger down. I remember when it had a
thimble on it."

Some of the Hollywood sets keep more or less to their own
group, never seeing anyone else, but this is no different from
other places. I remember the Philadelphia Main Liners who
always used to take a ducal shooting lodge in Scotland in
summer, taking with them the very same people they saw
every day at home. (One friend of mine who usually went
on these shooting parties was living for a time in a hotel in
Philadelphia and decided late at night to take a bath. He was
enjoying himself, singing lustily in the tub, when a call
came from downstairs that the people in the next room were
protesting that they couldn't sleep. "Tell them to read," said
the Philadelphian.)

What I minded about my brothers coming to Hollywood
was that I felt it was such a loss for the public. Jack and

Lionel had both been superb in the theater. To think that Jack could be the great Hamlet and then to see him in endless *Something Loves* was distressing. I always longed to see him play *Richard II.* I don't think he was ever satisfied. I don't think yachts and swimming pools make up for other things. Perhaps he always had a feeling that Mummum was looking down, disapprovingly. There was a great bond there.

In California one of my pleasant experiences was going with Somerset Maugham to see the movies in the different projection rooms when he came to do some supervising on the writing of the script for *The Razor's Edge.* He stayed at George Cukor's house and, while there, as he always does, he started writing every morning at eight o'clock and kept at it for four hours. He has become a warmer person than when I first knew him—I feel it is a real privilege to have become a friend of his.

People kept trying, of course, to get me to go back to the theater. Once when they wanted me to play *The Madwoman of Chaillot,* the pressure was so high that I went to Phoenix, Arizona, to escape it. Nobody knew where I was going but I was no sooner inside the door than the telephone rang and Mr. de Liagre was asking to speak to Miss Barrymore. But I didn't yield to either pressure or persuasion. I liked Mr. de Liagre enormously, and I thought the play had brilliance, but I just didn't want to do it and I didn't.

I went back to New York for the birth of my daughter's baby, and Britt, who had sat on the steps of the porch at Mamaroneck when Sister was being born upstairs, drove Sister and her baby and me home from the hospital.

I have always been happy that I had my children at home.

ETHEL BARRYMORE
IN 'A. N. T. A. ALBUM'

Star Agrees to Portray Role of Kate in 'Twelve Pound Look' at Benefit Here Jan. 29

By LOUIS CALTA

Ethel Barrymore has agreed to appear in the latest edition, the third, of the "ANTA Album," the theatre industry's annual benefit for itself, which is to be held at the Ziegfeld Theatre on Sunday evening, Jan. 29.

The celebrated 70-year-old performer, last seen on Broadway five years ago in "Embezzled Heaven," will portray once more her famous role of Kate in the late Sir James M. Barrie's "The Twelve Pound Look."

The four-character one-actor, one of Miss Barrymore's favorite plays, second only to "Peter Pan," will be done in its entirety. The Barrie work was first produced by the late Charles Frohman on Feb. 13, 1911, at the Empire Theatre as a curtain-raiser for "Alice-Sit-by-the-Fire." The bill ran locally for only thirty-two performances, but Miss Barrymore toured with it for many years captivating audiences throughout the country and in London.

(*New York Times,* December 29, 1949)

Every now and then I go back to New York to see Sister and the baby. Once when the American National Theatre and Academy heard I was coming, they asked me to do *The Twelve Pound Look* at their annual benefit and I said I would.

For years I had been carrying on the same typewriter in the play, a small light one, but Eddie McHugh, my stage manager, had sent it to his home in South Dakota so ANTA provided one for the performance.

It weighed nine thousand pounds, when I came on the stage carrying it. The whole audience stood up. The applause lasted over five minutes and that is a long, long time for applause to last. And do you know what happened to that great heavy typewriter during those five minutes? It got lighter and lighter, and I just tossed it on the table.

After the play there were many, many curtain calls. I was always much too shy to make curtain speeches, but this night I felt that I must at least say thank you and I added, "You make it very tempting."

Except for those few journeys back to see Sister and Johnny, and my younger son, Jackie, I have kept on living in California, making motion pictures and sometimes appearing on television and radio. I have always hoped that I could interest someone in Hollywood in making the Book of Ruth. Instead of making spectacular Biblical pictures, I wanted them to make a spectacularly simple Biblical picture which would be the Book of Ruth, where the principal expense would be two donkeys and a sickle. There is even a love story there.

For several years at Easter I read the Passion Story from St. Matthew on the *Family Theater* for Father Peyton. It always brought me thousands of letters from Protestants as well as Catholics, including one that deeply touched me from M. A. De Wolfe Howe. He said that he had just happened to be listening to the radio that night and although he had thought he had been hearing St. Matthew all his life, he had never really heard him before.

And once after I was no longer doing the readings, I happened accidentally to turn on my radio one Sunday in spring, just in time to hear myself reading that Easter story —the only time, I think, that I have ever heard a recording of my voice. Oh dear!

I have never seen any of the motion pictures in which I have appeared. When people ask me why, I laugh and say, "Oh, let me have my dream."

It seems strange that one's memory in later years should turn more toward things that are far in the past, that things which happened fifty years ago seem nearer and more real and more important than those which happened yesterday. Looking back, I discover, rather to my astonishment and disappointment, that I have never been able to bear malice toward anybody, although there have been plenty of opportunities for it.

For me there are some autumn memories as clear and bright as any remembrance of spring. One is of the day when New York University gave me an honorary degree. There were thousands and thousands of graduates sitting on the grass on the hillside as far as the eye could see. When I was given my degree, they all stood up. In the sunlight, wearing the different-colored hoods and tassels of their various arts and sciences, they looked like a field of flowers.

And the other, and the best one of all, is of my seventieth birthday.

Under the auspices of The Academy of Motion Picture Arts and Sciences of which he is president, my old, dear

New York University

Presentation, Citation and Investiture of
Ethel Barrymore
with the Honorary Degree of
Doctor of Fine Arts

Ethel Barrymore, great lady of the American theatre, is presented for the degree of Doctor of Fine Arts. Born in Philadelphia, schooled in the quiet of the Convent on Rittenhouse Square, her early disposition toward a career in music was summarily dispelled by an ancestral calling. For over two hundred years her family has been conspicuously identified with the stage. From the bassinet in her mother's dressing room in the theatre, to the throne of long reigning queen of the Drew-Barrymore dynasty, her tour of the hearts of the theatre-loving public has been an uninterrupted processional of glory in crescendo. The magnetism, the witchery, the power of her personality infallibly enchant us. Her versatile personifications are the more vivid because throughout them all she best personifies Ethel Barrymore. For her personal family devotion no less than her superlative contributions to the precious architecture of make believe, we adore her, and so welcome her into this academic communion with fervent satisfaction.

Vice Chancellor and Secretary

Ethel Barrymore, in gratitude for the life-giving radiance from the theatrical firmament which you so bountifully bestow upon an age that sorely needs such sustenance we gladly admit you to the honors implicit in the degree of Doctor of Fine Arts.

Chancellor

Dated June 11, 1952

friend, Charles Brackett, arranged and presided over a nation-wide broadcast in which my friends, old and new, said things about me for all the country to hear—and for me to hear.

I cannot think of any better way to end the story of my life than to share, with those who have been sharing in my

ETHEL BARRYMORE IS HONORED AT 70

Truman Among 100 Admirers to Congratulate Her in Pre-Recorded Radio Program

By THOMAS F. BRADY
Special to THE NEW YORK TIMES.

HOLLYWOOD, Calif., Aug. 15 - Ethel Barrymore, doyenne of the American stage and screen, received congratulations by radio tonight on her seventieth birthday from nearly 100 friends and admirers, headed by President Truman. The messages and felicitations were broadcast in a half-hour, pre-recorded program over the ABC network scheduled for release at 10:30 o'clock in each time zone across the country.

(*New York Times*, August 16, 1949)

sorrows and my rejoicings, as they read this book, the last, deep happiness of coming suddenly upon this unsuspected image of myself as others see me.

If to share this happiness seems like vanity, I am sorry; it is not in vanity but in humblest thankfulness that I am offering to share it.

To share the sound of Bing Crosby's voice, singing "Happy Birthday" . . .

To listen with me to the tributes of President Truman and Mr. Herbert Hoover . . .

To hear the dear, remembered voices of a hundred other friends, each bringing its own echo of that birthday message from all the corners of the earth . . .

And Katharine Hepburn saying, as only her voice could say it:

. . . I think what astounds us people of the screen and theater about her is the number and intensity of her interests. Would it be disloyal to my profession for me to hint that great stars are apt to show a little more interest in themselves than in anything else? Not Miss Barrymore. It's the world she's interested in—or rather a lot of different worlds—sports, history, music, politics, books. It seems impossible that a human being with the austere allowance of only twenty-four hours every day can keep in such close touch with them.

She has more friends than anyone I know, but she's not a dear, gentle soul. Barrymores don't come like that. She has a trenchant wit, she can rebuke stupidity, or intolerance with silence better than Joe Louis could do it with his fists. She makes appallingly accurate observations. She doesn't know the meaning of fear or the meaning of caution . . .

And Arthur Hopkins telling about the family tradition and inheritance, and Lionel, with memories of Mummum and of our father and mother and Uncle Jack . . .

And Ruth Gordon reading that excitedly extravagant review of *Captain Jinks* that I have already quoted . . .

And Lucile Watson remembering back to 1903 when she received a telegram from me on her opening night, saying:

. . . I saw all those wonderful plays of hers, and was in several of them. And from her I learned an important lesson in acting: When thousands came nightly to be thrilled by her magnetic voice, I was watching something else—the way she listened to the speeches of her fellow players, and I thank her now for any knowledge I have of what is perhaps the highest art of an actor—the art of beautiful listening. . . .

And Katharine Cornell . . . And Walter Hampden . . . And Billie Burke:

The first time I met you, Ethel darling, was in London, in 1906. You were crossing the lobby of the Carleton on your way to some ducal dinner party. . . . The following year Mr. Frohman brought me to New York to be the leading lady with your Uncle John Drew. There was a difficulty, however. John Drew thought Billie an undignified name for his leading lady. Perhaps he thought I should expand it to Wilhelmina. I didn't want to, but I had no idea how to win my point. Mr. Frohman had asked you to take me to our first rehearsal, to break the ice and you did, and by your magic I remained Billie. . . . Happy Birthday, Ethel. . . .

And Elsie Janis, with one last inimitable imitation of my voice . . . And Alfred Lunt . . . And Lynn Fontanne:

When I came to America, you were among the first people I met. I was an unknown actress and there was no reason that you should have said more than how do you do, but you did. You were kind and friendly and I've never forgotten. When I met Alfred, one of the more endearing acts of his courtship was when he rushed me to see the woman he loved, in a matinee. You were playing *Déclassée*.

And Tallulah Bankhead:

I'm sorry, darlings, but *Déclassée* is my cue. I'm the all-time authority on *Déclassée*. I saw Ethel Barrymore play Lady Helen Haden thirteen times. Just up from Alabama and suffering from economic cramps more often than not, I saw it from a perpendicular stance at the rear of the theater. Ethel Barrymore was then forty, eighteen years of stardom behind her. At forty I thought that she was the most exciting actress, the most vivid personality I had ever seen on the stage. The lapse of thirty years has not changed that juvenile conviction. At seventy I still think that Ethel Barrymore is the most exciting actress, the most vivid personality I have ever seen on the stage. Over the last half century in the American theater it hasn't been hard to find Ethel Barrymore if you knew where to look for her at its top, its very, very top. It may have been a little lonely up there at times, but the peak was and is her rightful residence in the theater. I love you, Ethel.

And Spencer Tracy:

The year 1924. The play, *A Royal Fandango.* You, Miss Barrymore, were the star. I had one line. On the opening night I stood waiting for my entrance, shakily wondering whom they'd get to replace me the second night. Suddenly you stopped beside me and said quietly, "Relax. That's all you have to do—just relax." This is Spencer Tracy. I've been capitalizing on that advice ever since.

And other heartwarming messages, from Claudette Colbert and Gregory Peck and Cary Grant . . .

And Somerset Maugham, remembering me in *Lady Frederick* and *The Constant Wife*:

When Ethel Barrymore played the leading role in *Lady Frederick*, she was in the prime of her youth and beauty which the passage of years has left unspoiled. She played the part of a middle-aged woman, and it is surely a tribute to her wonderful gifts that young and beautiful as she was, she persuaded the audience to believe that she had seen her best days. . . .

In *The Constant Wife* there was one line which I shall never forget. It wasn't even a line. It was a single word, the word "when." I had written it because it was the natural, obvious word for the heroine of my play to say, and it had never occurred to me that there was anything more in it than the inquiry it made. But Ethel Barrymore put such a wealth of meaning, humor, innuendo and malice—none of which I had seen—into that little word that the audience rocked with laughter until I thought they'd never stop. It just shows you what a great actress can do when the author gives her half a chance. If I hadn't fallen madly in love with Ethel during the rehearsals, I should have fallen in love with her then. . . .

And Mrs. Franklin Delano Roosevelt . . . And dear Bernie Baruch, using to describe me my own line from *Sunday*:

Ethel Barrymore—that's all there is. There isn't any more . . .

And Herbert Bayard Swope:

This thing is all wrong. This date has fallen into the hands of the chronologists who want to mark the seventieth year of Ethel Barrymore's *age*. That's silly. Ethel has no age. She is an unchanging and unchangeable spirit. There is in her today the same fire, the same charm, the same alertness and the same ability to make those she meets glow and thrill at seeing her that she had when I first became her willing subject, and that was one day when I, as a young reporter, saw her for the first time. She was with Richard Harding Davis, in front of the old Weber and Fields Music Hall. She then had that utterly irresistible attraction. She has it today: She will always have it. . . .

And a cable from Strasbourg, signed "Winston" . . . And Zoë Akins' birthday poem "Quatrain for Ethel":

What is she like? I'd say the orange tree
That at the same time gives both fruit and flower;
For though the yield is rich, this very hour
Is perfumed by the harvest yet to be.

And then Lionel:

It's time for the family now, Ethel. The one who has known you ever since you first opened your eyes wants to wish you happy birthday for the seventieth time, and here are some young people you have known ever since they opened their eyes—maybe a little longer.

And Sammy: "Happy Birthday, Mother!"

And Jackie: "Happy Birthday, Mother Darling!"

And Sister: "Happy Birthday, Mama! And here's another generation, John Drew Miglietta."

And Johnny: "Happy Birthday, Mummum!"

And my answer to them all—and to all of you—

Thank you, Johnny darling, and thank you children. Thank you Mr. President, and all my friends. I am afraid there's not enough time left in my life in which to tell you all of my gratitude and appreciation for this overwhelming tribute. It is much more than I deserve, but please believe me, it is not more than I can take to my heart. Thank you.

But my story does not end with any word of mine. It ends with Johnny saying "Happy Birthday, Mummum!"
Mummum!

*

Since I have finished this book Lionel has died. I like to think that he and Jack are together—and that they will be glad to see me.

E. B.

Index